WORKING
WITH
ETHNICITY, RACE
AND CULTURE
IN MENTAL HEALTH

WORKING WITH ETHNICITY, RACE AND CULTURE IN MENTAL HEALTH

A HANDBOOK FOR PRACTITIONERS

HÁRI SEWELL

JESSICA KINGSLEY PUBLISHERS
LONDON AND PHILADELPHIA

First published in 2009
by Jessica Kingsley Publishers
116 Pentonville Road
London N1 9JB, UK
and
400 Market Street, Suite 400
Philadelphia, PA 19106, USA

www.jkp.com

Copyright © Hári Sewell 2009

For further information please visit www.harisewell.com

Library of Congress Cataloging in Publication Data
A CIP catalog record for this book is available from the Library of Congress

British Library Cataloguing in Publication Data
A CIP catalogue record for this book is available from the British Library

ISBN 978 1 84310 621 0

Printed and bound in Great Britain by
Athenaeum Press, Gateshead, Tyne and Wear

To Jacqui Dillon, my Rock. My constant. Thank you for creating so much from so little.

To my precious and absolutely stunning sons James-Earl and Aaron. Thank you for giving me so much love and support to get to the end of this project.

Dara and Sia. Thank you for the affection and the space.

Lorenzo and Hazel Sewell. You are the explanation most people seek from me.

ACKNOWLEDGEMENTS

Thanks to my colleagues who have rehearsed these ideas with me for 15 years. Your influences are reflected here: Errol Francis, Sue Holland, Suman Fernando, Yvonne Christie, Melba Wilson, Sharon Jennings, Sandra Griffiths, Malcolm Phillips, Frank Keating, Parimala Moodley, Lennox Thomas, Olivia Nuamah, Kwame McKenzie, Barbara D'Gamma.

To those who were critical in setting high standards: Martin Smith, Jo Cleary.

And to Francesca Russo, Peter Gilbert, James Sandham and Geoff Alltimes.

CONTENTS

TABLES

FIGURES

FOREWORD

The past few years have seen many books commenting on the failure of mental health services to meet the needs of black and minority ethnic people. Some highlight the effects of racism – especially 'institutional racism' – while others emphasise the lack of sensitivity to cultural difference in the ways of working, especially the 'medical model' of (Western) psychiatry on which services are generally based. Government plans to address the problems top-down appear to try riding both horses, but all too often fall between them or fall off both.

What is happening at the coal face of mental health care is that professionals are left searching for ways forward, trying to meet the proper and just expectations of culturally diverse service users, trying not to be racist in practice, and endeavouring to improve the quality of service that they provide. Going back to school, studying the faults in the systems they are supposed to work with, analysing their own capabilities, undergoing training to become 'culturally competent' (whatever that means) and so on, are not really options for most busy people under pressure. They have to make do, learn a bit about issues to do with race, ethnicity and culture, how an ideal system should work and try to understand how their own practices can contribute to ensuring that the service is improved for everyone. This is where this book by Hári Sewell comes in. This is a book for practitioners – essentially a self-training book but also one that could be used as a source of knowledge in a complex and controversial field.

The author knows about the realities at the grass roots, how NHS mental health care is currently set up, what types of approach are practicable and what are not and he understands what busy practitioners may look for in a book called a 'handbook'. What he has done is to digest the literature, think about matters, connect with service users, talk with managers and professionals and then provide readers with a succinct account geared towards helping practitioners to change their practice – indicating how and why these changes can make a real difference.

This book discusses all the main aspects of terms used in the field of mental health care in relation to a culturally and racially diverse population. It then delves into practical matters – assessments, recovery focused care and so on, providing clear practical guidance on implementation, illustrated by concrete examples from real life and many case descriptions. Most importantly the book provides evidence and a rationale for every suggestion that is made, indicating the author's wide ranging knowledge and grasp of the topics discussed. The tables and illustrations help to focus effectively on the main aspects of what the author is trying to convey. This is a book directed to people working at ground level in mental health services where the action takes place – a very practical book informed by common sense, a wealth of knowledge and clear thinking.

Dr Suman Fernando,
European Centre for Migration and Social Care (MASC),
University of Kent.

CHAPTER 1

WHAT IS 'ETHNICITY, RACE AND CULTURE'?

Language conveys many things; some intended and others not. An attempt to achieve precision in the use of terms specific to any area of study can be viewed as pedantic or futile. Terminology develops as a means to establish a shared understanding but people intend or hear different meanings. This chapter sets out definitions of ethnicity, race and culture (ERC). The aim is to establish a common understanding between author and reader about the intended meanings for terms used in this book.

A lack of precision in understanding terms and concepts leads to confusion and poorer response to need. For example, a focus on culture in a context where race (and racism) is the issue, fails to address the real problem appropriately.

Definitions

Fernando (1991) provides a succinct description of the difference between ethnicity race and culture. His helpful chart is reproduced in Table 1.1:

Table 1.1 Race, ethnicity and culture

	Characterised by	Determined by	Perceived as
Race	Physical appearance	Genetic ancestry	Permanent (genetic / biological)
Culture	Behaviour Attitudes	Upbringing Choice	Changeable (assimilation, acculturation)
Ethnicity	Sense of belonging Group identity	Social pressures Psychological need	Partially changeable

(Fernando 1991, p.11)

Cashmore and Troyna (1990) provide a useful glossary including definitions of less frequently used terms such as colonialism and social Darwin-
ism. Many contemporary writers in the field of mental health provide
helpful insights into the distinction between terms (e.g. Bhugra and Bhui
2002; Moodley and Palmer 2006).

Race

Race is the most fundamental of the terms to be considered because of the
historical backdrop of systematic forms of racial oppression, for example
slavery. Race was considered to be fixed through biology, however as
science progressed it has become clear that the old assumptions about race
were inaccurate. Arguments have been made since the early 20th century
that the biological basis for the division of humans into races is flawed
(Banton 1967). Rack (1982) sets out persuasive arguments for dismantling
the concept that races are well-defined groups of people who are biologi-
cally and genetically alike. The genetic differences within so-called racial
groups are sometimes greater than those between people of different races.
There is no complete set of genetic characteristics that defines a race (Senior
and Bhopal 1994). Therefore the use of *race* as a reliable biogenetic divide is
flawed. Race cannot reliably be used to provide a genetic explanation for
trends and patterns (Bhopal 1997). The main benefits of applying the
concept of race are social (Banton 1967).

The distinction being made here is that science is based on the pursuit
of reliability and certainty. The genetic concept of race cannot provide this;
in the social world, however, interactions between people based on assumptions about race serve the purpose of stratifying global and national populations (Altman 2006; Banton 1965). It serves societies well to continue to
promote the concept of race and to accentuate difference as it creates a social
order.

Many social and economic concerns about disparities associated with
race could potentially be tackled by considering class as the salient charac-
teristic (Alexander 1987). This would perhaps be more honest as it would
apply social analysis to social ills as opposed to the use of a term that implies
a scientific coherence where there is none. People are attacked and killed
because of their perceived race so though class does provide a paradigm it
does not hold all the answers.

This discussion is clearly not a theoretical argument about whether or
not *race* exists. It is absolutely apparent in injustices of everyday life and in
the more extreme cases of murder, that race does exist. It is important,
however, that people in mental health services understand that the patterns
and trends that seem to relate to race are at best seen as a negative conse-

quence of how people are initially perceived. Searches for biological explanations have failed (McKenzie and Chakroborty 2003). Of the three terms being explored here (ERC), race is the one that is considered to be within the person and fixed (see Table 1.1). In practice it is utilised as a signifier for ethnicity and/or culture and, erroneously, for class (Williams 1997).

BOX 1.1 ILLUSTRATION

A black man in his mid-twenties is being assessed. He appears to be black African or African Caribbean. His ancestry is in fact part South American and part Caribbean. He was brought up in an upper-middle-class environment in Ecuador, has a university degree and has a strong South American identity. When assessed in the English mental health services for the first time the social worker considers race as part of the process. The physical appearance of this man, i.e. that he is black, offers no reliable or useful information other than the knowledge that he is probably perceived as having particular experiences and attributes because he looks black. It is the relationship between his blackness and society that creates meaning. His ethnic identity will in its own right bring richer information, which will include his 'race' as well as culture, geographical heritage, language and religion.

Race is important because it affects how people are perceived, including the ascribing of a range of stereotypes. The ascribing stereotypes based on race is not something that is only done by white people. People within minority groups often hold negative stereotypes about their own ethnic group and will have a split created within themselves where they seek to have a positive sense of self whilst seeing their ethnicity as representative of negative attributes. Fanon (1967) describes very well the internalisation of the negative stereotypes. People of different backgrounds will perceive race as having some meaning because in essence race is shorthand, a cipher, for other assumptions ascribed through national and global socialisation processes.

Racism, that is discrimination on the basis of race (rather than ethnicity or culture), is an emotive subject as was evident around the launch of the government's response to the Blofeld report of the investigation into the care and treatment of David 'Rocky' Bennett (NSCSTHA 2003). Government ministers were asked by the inquiry panel and some leaders in the field of race and mental health to accept the finding of the panel that the

National Health Service (NHS) was institutionally racist. This position was never adopted by the government though senior officials in the Department of Health had said, in response to the inquiry panel's questioning, that the NHS was institutionally racist. Ministers stated that discrimination was present in the NHS but refused to use the term 'institutionally racist' (*Guardian* 2005). This illustration highlights the sensitivity around race being the focus of discrimination.

Government audits and research findings highlight that the poorest experiences and outcomes of black and minority ethnic (BME) groups in mental health services relate to people from African and African Caribbean backgrounds (the African Diaspora) (Commission for Healthcare Audit and Inspection 2007a). This broad sweep of people with heritages in the second largest continent and a raft of islands are united singularly in the fact that they are perceived as belonging to the same race (rather than ethnic or cultural group). It stands to reason that if it can be accepted that discrimination occurs (which the government did) and that this consistently has a particular impact on people who are considered as belonging to a single race, the specific type of discrimination is racial discrimination.

The reluctance to accept a charge of racism may reflect a decoupling of closely related concepts. Bhugra and Bhui (2002) point out that racism, as opposed to racial discrimination, is more rooted in the ideological belief in the inferiority of races. Though racial discrimination may not be driven by individuals who consciously hold these beliefs, institutional racism is the consequence of the individual's unwitting acts (see Figure 1.1 later in this chapter).

Mixed heritage

Each decade sees a massive upturn in international travel, interracial relationships and the erosion of the notion of three distinct races, however, Post-Darwinian classifications of the races into black, Asian and white have remained current (Cashmore and Troyna 1990). Banton (1967) conducted a study of the history of racial categorisations of humans, beginning with the work of Aristotle. His conclusions were that a primary function of race is to create social stratification manifested as racism, with the power of white people over all others creating the clearest divide. In an echo of his study Okitikpi (2005a) argues that racially the world is considered to be binary; people are either white or they are not! In Western societies and in urban areas in particular, however, there are many variations to perceived races and ethnicities. This means that old classifications are too narrow to capture the true heritage of people in mental health services (Hall 1996).

In mental health provision a failure to acknowledge the unique experiences of people from mixed heritage weakens assessments and limits the analysis of problems. The need to consider mixed heritage in its own right is discussed in Chapter 6. In the illustration in Box 1.1 the man considered to be black was in fact of mixed heritage. Based on physical characteristics alone assumptions can easily be made and attributes ascribed erroneously.

In summary, the physical characteristics of race tell us little more than the fact that someone is likely to have experienced discrimination on the basis of this attribute.

Ethnicity

Ethnicity encapsulates a range of factors used to identify individuals and may relate to language, geographical origin, skin colour, religion and cultural practices. As such, ethnicity is not a fixed or easily definable concept. Stuart Hall (1996) argues that in multicultural Britain new ethnicities are being developed. Ethnicity therefore can be fluid and is based largely on self-definition. As such, the term is not easily subjected to inflexible definitions (Senior and Bhopal 1994). For a practitioner, the ethnicity of service users is a gateway to issues that they consider to be relevant to their identity: who they are, how they live and their relationship with services.

The term 'ethnicity' has its roots in a Greek word for people or tribe (Senior and Bhopal 1994). Ethnic group and ethnic origin have been defined differently. Ethnic origin is fixed and pertains to religion, language, geography, physical appearance and the culture associated with these factors. Ethnic group is self-defined though is usually related to the aforementioned characteristics (Bhopal 1997; Department of Health 2005a).

Self-definition means that the potential richness of information cannot be inferred but must come from further exploration with the service user. Ethnicity is not neutral. Modood *et al.* (1998) highlight the various and extensive aspects of life in which minority ethnic groups experience disadvantage. Hall (1996) discusses the loaded notion of 'difference' and the fact that ideas about race and ethnicity are yet to be decoupled. Further to the actual disadvantage experienced by people from BME backgrounds, an association is created with negative factors, as is the case for race. In seeking to break these associations, Williams (1997) states that 'race is not a cipher for…poverty…disease…bestiality…the subhuman…exotic entertainment' (pp.60–61).

The term 'minority ethnic group' most reliably conveys disadvantage and, often, inferiority (Bhopal 1997). These inferences affect people whether they are from within or outside a minority ethnic group.

'Minority ethnic groups' is a term developed around the 1980s following on from its inaccurate predecessor 'ethnic minority groups'. The problem with this earlier term is that it implies that 'minority groups' are ethnic; the assumption being that only 'different' people have an ethnic identity. In Western societies this would equate to white people being ethnicity-free. This is clearly not the case. All people have an ethnic identity. The current description makes it clear that those being referred to are ethnic groups that together or singularly are in the minority in a society. In some societies, such as on the African continent, white communities are in the minority. It is striking, however, that the term 'minority ethnic group' does not have global transferability in terms of its negative inferences. Wright (2006) illustrates that wherever white and black communities live in close proximity, white people always have the superior or dominant position. Though new regimes in South Africa or Zimbabwe may appear to counter this assertion, proportionally more white people per head of population still retain privilege and wealth and though in the minority, still attract deference from many black citizens.

The term 'minority ethnic groups' does not describe a homogenous collective (Sewell 2004). A Japanese woman and a West African man are so ethnically different that it is not possible to develop a service response supposedly tailored to universally meet the needs of people from BME groups.

Modood *et al.* 1998 takes this a step further by showing in detail the variations in socio-economic experience and outcome of different minority groups in Britain. The study shows the differences in the disparities across ethnic groups in relation to such matters as housing, employment and education. Effective practitioners in mental health will need to inform their assessment and practice with detailed information from the service user point of view. Service users hold the key as to the factors that they see as relevant in their own identity. Beyond this ability to explore identity and cultural issues from a service user perspective, a practitioner will need to understand empirical information. Much information is available about the impact of ethnicity on the experience of living in Britain and specifically about interactions with mental health services. Chapter 2 highlights the hard evidence for considering ERC as distinct issues in mental health.

It is clear that the term 'minority ethnic group' is useful only in signifying that there is likely to be some form of differential experience and outcome and that this needs to be explored. All assessments are in fact strengthened by detailed consideration of identity and an understanding of the empirical information relating to a person's ethnic group.

Culture

Like ethnicity, culture is considered to be changeable. Culture is described as the substance of cohesion between people. It represents shared ideas, non-material structures, habits and rules that help to circumscribe membership of a group (Bhui 2002; Fernando 1991). Culture, simply put, means way of life (Fernando 1995). Fernando (1991, p.10) states that 'partly because of its lack of precision culture is often confused with race'. Bhui (2002, p.16) states, 'most modern societies are mixtures of many sub-cultures'.

Culture will shift and change as groups interact with each other. Technology alters human behaviour and migration influences everyday living. As Fernando (1995, p.5) states, 'cultures are not static, especially in a community where there are people from several cultures living side by side'.

Application to practice

Practitioners in mental health will find that they are accused of being reductionist or stereotypical if they seek to define cultures as if they are fixed and suited to cataloguing. A statement in absolute terms about what any group of people is like is prone to overlook individuals. As a *predictor* of personal preferences, cultural knowledge is likely to be fundamentally flawed and is the antithesis of person-centred care. It is often advantageous, however, to have cultural knowledge as an *indicator* of what might be relevant. Cultural knowledge may enable useful questions to be asked and will on occasions prevent offence or embarrassment being caused unwittingly.

One problem with seeking to learn about an unfamiliar culture in any way other than experiencing it is that the passing on of information requires a deconstruction of complex and intricate generalisations. Defining statements about a specific culture can only be accurate if they include moderators such as 'it is common', 'usually' or 'often'. At best, stereotypes or individualised perceptions are presented as norms and at worst the person relaying the information may use it as a means of promoting what they feel *should* be the cultural norm.

There are so many influences on culture that it is a challenge for anyone outside of the culture to understand the norm based on Limited Acquired Cultural Knowledge (LACK) (Sewell 2004). Responding to cultural needs therefore becomes fraught with problems from a practitioner point of view. Not only is culture a nebulous concept; it is also barely reliably (or universally) defined by those within it.

Culture is perceived as being less emotive than race. Fernando (1991) and Cashmore and Troyna (1990) make the point effectively in reference to the speech by the Prime Minster Margaret Thatcher in 1982 in which she refers to Britain being swamped by other cultures. Had the Prime Minister stated that Britons were concerned about being swamped by other *races* the intensity of the reaction would have been greater; not because the sentiment would have had no currency in 1980s Britain but because the mention of race makes a claim of racism less easy to avoid. Culture was used euphemistically for race, a position adopted by many interested in race politics in Britain at the time. Whatever the truth about inferences it is well recognised that culture evokes a less passionate debate than race.

Patricia Williams, in the Reith Lectures of 1997 articulates the potency of race well. The Reith Lectures are a series on BBC Radio 4 named after the first director general of the corporation. These enable prominent academics and leaders to lecture on their specialist subjects, enabling a wide audience to have access to a high degree of expertise and specialist knowledge.

> Conversations about race so quickly devolve into anxious bouts of wondering why we are not talking about something – anything – else, like hard work or personal responsibility or birth order or class or God or the good old glories of the human spirit. All these are worthy topics of conversation, surely, but can we consider for just one moment, race (Williams 1997, p.61)

In mental health services there are times when it is right to focus on culture and it does not just serve the function of avoiding race. There are broad cultural differences between social groups and these do have an impact on relationships and the perception of a shared identity. Differences in culture, whatever is included as descriptors, may lead to real differences in understandings and communication of certain experiences. This has been well argued in literature since the seminal works of Littlewood and Lipsedge 1989; Rack 1982 and Fernando 1991. It is important to remember that there are some people within a BME group who may adhere to practices that are codified as being 'cultural' and others who act or behave much less in accordance with these codes. For practitioners there is a risk that their understanding of a group's culture is defined by the practices of the strict, devout or traditional minority within it.

Practitioners are therefore faced with a challenge. Of the terms described in this chapter, culture is discussed and explored in society and in health and social care with the least emotion. Culture is often used euphemistically for race but is weak in terms of its specificity. The avoidance of focusing on race or minority ethnic groups takes attention off people and deals with culture, which is nebulous and intangible.

BOX 1.2 EXERCISE

Imagine you are an unseen observer in a training course in a country with a cultural heritage very different to your own. In this course a lecturer attempts to describe to the locals how people from your country or continent behave. In their description they refer to:

- eating patterns
- preferred diet
- typical social life
- major cultural preoccupations (e.g. typical conversations amongst acquaintances)
- specific tell-tale mannerisms or behaviours that distinguish your cultural group.

First, note down what you feel you might hear the lecturer say.

Second, note down on a scale of 1 to 5 the closeness of the descriptions to your own behaviour or experience with 1 representing the closest match and 5 the furthest.

The problem with race

A major Department of Health programme to work towards equality has the main title *Delivering Race Equality* (DRE) and this has been resourced and supported at very senior levels. DRE includes a number of elements, with training for staff being key amongst these (Department of Health 2005b). The premise behind the element on training is that staff sometimes treat people differently because of their race and that this has an adverse effect on outcomes. There continues therefore to be a breakdown in logic. A major programme of change is tackling inequality between races and there is an acceptance that behaviour of staff in mental health services may contribute to this but the subject of racism is avoided and its effect is even denied (e.g. in Singh and Burns 2006).

One powerful impact of focusing on ethnicity and culture is that it neutralises the language of discrimination. Terms for systematic and embedded forms of discrimination often have an adjective/noun that is derived from the infinitive or another root word. These derivatives cut through dialogue and provide a description of a person or behaviour in absolute terms. Someone is either racist or not. Frantz Fanon points to this absolute position in *Black Skin, White Masks* (Fanon 1967). All such descriptions of people or behaviour convey a statement of abhorrence. This may not always be helpful as it may mitigate against open discussion and exploration of personal prejudices. A benefit however is that the accurate use of terms is significant in problem-solving. A poorly defined problem leads to a poor solution.

The disruption of the ability to express discrimination precisely is illustrated in Table 1.2.

Table 1.2 Language of discrimination

Infinitive/Root	Adjective/Noun
Race	Racism/Racist
Sex (Gender)	Sexism/Sexist
Age	Ageism/Ageist
Sexuality	Homophobia/Homophobic
Nations	Xenophobia/Xenophobic
Disability	'Disablist' is a new term emerging
Ethnicity	There is no specific or absolute term. People are described as discriminatory on the basis of ethnicity – or racist
Culture	There is no specific term

Through the use of precise terms practitioners are afforded the opportunity to challenge themselves or to be challenged on specific agendas such as racism. Within the context of current health and social care parlance this opportunity is lost. As stated previously, failure to define the problem accurately leads to poor problem-solving.

Institutional racism

Emphasis is given to race and racism in this chapter because the patterns that affect people of African and African Caribbean heritage have a consistent impact that is regardless of massive variations in the culture, ethnicity or language of people so described. The greatest degree of disparity in service utilisation relates to this group. It is hard to see how race is overtaken by ethnicity or culture when the one consistent aspect in this disparate group is race.

The language of racism becomes confused because there is still a perception that racism is best understood as an act or behaviour perpetrated by an individual. Further, it is regarded as a conscious attempt to be discriminatory. Definitions of institutional racism illustrate that this type of discrimination comes in different forms (Carmichael and Hamilton 1967; Cashmore and Troyna 1990; MacPherson 1999). The black activist Stokely Carmichael coined the term 'institutional racism' in the 1960s (Carmichael and Hamilton 1967). As Tuitt (2004, p.45) points out, 'the term institutional racism is not new to the British lexicon, but is a term that has positively rolled off the tongue of officials, politicians and community activists since the racist murder of Stephen Lawrence'.

MacPherson and his colleagues defined intuitional racism in the Stephen Lawrence Inquiry report as follows:

> Institutional Racism consists of the collective failure of an organisation to provide an appropriate and professional service to people because of their colour, culture or ethnic origin. It can be seen or detected in processes, attitudes and behaviour that amount to discrimination through unwitting prejudice, ignorance, thoughtlessness and racist stereotyping which disadvantage minority ethnic people. (MacPherson 1999, p.28)

The Macpherson definition contains 55 words and this is beyond the natural recall for a lot of people. It can be simplified by focusing on the three key elements that underpin the MacPherson definition of institutional racism, i.e. that there are:

- collective failures

- unwitting attitudes and behaviours

- poorer outcomes for BME groups.

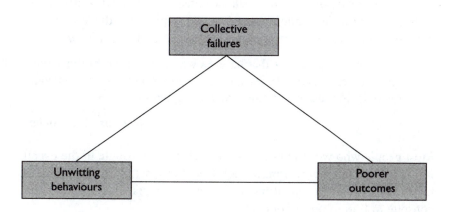

Figure 1.1 Institutional racism

The three elements need to be present for the concept of institutional racism to be applicable. If, for example, the processes, behaviour or attitudes were deliberate it would be regarded as systematic racism and would not fit this definition. If there were individual acts as opposed to a collective failure, again, the MacPherson definition would not hold.

The third element is that there is evidence of poorer outcomes. If an organisation does not measure outcomes for BME people even though trends and patterns repeatedly nationally and internationally indicate that these are likely to be poorer, this indicates a collective failure. Ignorance arising from the fact that its outcomes are not monitored and analysed does not mean that the poorer outcomes do not exist! Another critical aspect of the MacPherson definition of institutional racism that is not explicitly acknowledged is that it refers to minority ethnic groups and not just to race. It is not surprising therefore that confusion arises when the government accepts the MacPherson definition of institutional racism and accepts that there is discrimination (against minority ethnic groups – as stated in DRE) but refuses to accept that there is institutional racism. Further to the confusion caused, many black workers within mental health services are affected by the failure to acknowledge racism. This particular issue creates an unspoken fault line in the mental health workforce. This division is captured well by Williams (1997) when she describes 'the paralysing anxiety of well-meaning "white guilt" and the smouldering unhappiness of blacks who dare not speak their minds' (p.59).

A benefit of fully appreciating the definition is the clarification that, contrary to the interpretation made by some, it does not blame individual workers nor does it paint an organisation as evil. The paradox that occurred when the Secretary of State for Health avoided using the term 'institutional racism' is that the description he used was a paraphrase of the MacPherson definition. In a written statement to Members of Parliament he wrote:

> Behaviours and processes that have grown up in mental health services mean that there is particular inequity in the provision of care and outcomes for people from black and ethnic minority groups.

> (*Guardian* 2004, online)

Most people who work in mental health services contribute to the overall impact of institutional racism, though few, if any, set out intending to be racist. It is often the unwitting behaviours and practices that together conspire to lead to poorer outcomes.

Nomenclature – black and minority ethnic groups

The term 'black and minority ethnic groups' is used routinely in modern literature. It refers to all people of minority ethnic backgrounds and includes white groups such as the Irish. There is a growing body of evidence that highlights the inequality of experience and outcome of Irish people, as discussed in Chapter 2 (Keating, Robertson and Kotecha 2003).

Modood *et al.* 1998 highlight the heterogeneity of the collective 'BME groups'. The language of 'minority ethnic groups' does not fully acknowledge that many of the people being described as such were born in the UK and regard themselves as Londoners, Glaswegian or British. Identity cannot be imposed. In this book the phrase 'people from BME backgrounds' is more frequently (though not exclusively) used to demonstrate that for some it is their heritage and consequential identity that leads to their inclusion within the definition.

People from African and African Caribbean backgrounds are sometimes referred to as 'black'. Throughout this book the term black is used exclusively in relation to this group.

The term 'African Diaspora' is occasionally used as an alternative to 'black'. This is done to emphasise that, despite the cultural variation between many groups described collectively as 'black', the connection goes back to Africa. The dispersal of peoples to the Caribbean and Americas and across Europe was primarily a function of slavery. Fryer (1984) makes this point in referring to black people trafficked to Britain as 'necessary implements'. The relationship between slavery and mental health is returned to at various points in this book.

Conclusion

The words and concepts employed when discussing ethnicity, race and culture are sometimes used without due consideration for their particular meanings. It is important to define the problem accurately when trying to address the disparities in experience and outcomes of people from BME backgrounds in mental health services. Ethnic and cultural differences do contribute to some differences but racism also is a cause. Racism is considered to be emotive and generates anxiety and avoidance, which in turn lead to attempts to tackle disparities in mental health services without honestly including the possibility of racism in the analysis of causes. Other potential causes of disparities should be considered but if racism is avoided solutions will be only partial and both service users and staff will remain unconvinced about the seriousness with which those in charge of services are seeking solutions.

CHAPTER 2

WHY ARE ETHNICITY, RACE AND CULTURE IMPORTANT IN MENTAL HEALTH SERVICES?

Legislation and policy

During a training session on race and mental health in 1993 a white community psychiatric nurse said that she did not 'get into all that stuff' as it would make her job too difficult (i.e. taking account of ethnic, racial and cultural needs of service users). Her comments indicated that she behaved as though this element of practice was optional. This was a racist view. It has always been the case that practitioners have an obligation to take into account the whole person. This includes their racial, ethnic and cultural background.

The Race Relations (Amendment) Act 2000 requires services to develop a Race Equality Scheme (RES) to show how they will fulfil their statutory duties. These duties are: to promote equality of opportunity; to eliminate unfair racial discrimination; and to promote good relations between all ethnic groups. The Race Relations Act (Amendment) 2000 is the successor to the Race Relations Act 1976, which outlawed racial discrimination in Britain. The law on its own does not, however, act as a deterrent except for when there is a high probability of prosecution or sanctions for breaking it. Sanctions for services may include a judicial review, the loss of contracts or penalisation by a regulatory body. In reality the risks are minimal.

National policy and Department of Health guidance places a requirement on services to respond to the needs of people from BME backgrounds and to eliminate or reduce disadvantage. The major policy framework for mental health is *Delivering Race Equality in Mental Health Care* (Department of Health 2005b). This includes three building blocks:

- better information

- community engagement

- more appropriate and responsive services.

The policy goes on to state 12 characteristics that services would have if it was successfully implemented. These include:

- Less fear of mental health services among BME communities and service users;

- Increased satisfaction with services;

- A reduction in the rate of admission of people from BME communities to psychiatric inpatient units;

- A reduction in the disproportionate rates of compulsory detention of BME service users in inpatient units'

The policing of compliance with policy or legislation falls to regulatory bodies. The Healthcare Commission and the Commission for Social Care Inspection along with the Mental Health Act of Commission are to combine to form the Care Quality Commission. This new body will operate in shadow form from October 2008 and begin substantive operation in April 2009 (Department of Health 2008a). Foundation Trusts perform against legally binding contracts. The organisation that regulates foundation trusts (called Monitor) operates a 'light touch' performance management approach. This relies on foundation trusts reporting when there are exceptions to the agreed standards and targets rather than routinely reporting against all performance indicators. This management by exception does not reduce the expectation on foundation trusts to meet their contractual obligations.

Third-sector organisations (also known as voluntary sector organisations) will be required by commissioners to meet objectives to deliver race equality in contracts or service level agreements. Most funders, including those independent of Department of Health policy requirements, will place some duty on providers to comply with the Race Relations (Amendment) Act 2000.

Most service providers and practitioners would not consider that taking account of racial, ethnic or cultural needs is an optional extra but there is little evidence-based information about what it means to do so effectively. Those in charge of organisations need to know and be convinced of the following:

- the causes, scale and implications of variations

- the extent to which mental health services are able to make a difference

- that they have a responsibility to do so.

The causes, scale and implications of variations

There are some gross variations and inequalities in the experience and outcomes for people from BME backgrounds in mental health services. Other variations may not be significant in terms of degree of disparity but still require a response.

However, many organisations and teams do not know the nature and scale of variations within their own services. Hypotheses vary about the cause of disparities in service utilisation and this sometimes spills over into public conflict. There have been claims and counter-claims on this subject by prominent psychiatrists and academics in the *British Journal of Psychiatry* (see, for example, Freeman 2003; McKenzie and Bhui 2007; McKenzie and Chakroborty 2003; Singh and Burns 2006). On 21 May 2007 the British Broadcasting Corporation current affairs programme *Newnight* led to some pointed arguments in which Professor Singh stated that the high rate of diagnosed psychosis in black groups was not as a result of racism. This led to claims that he was setting the debate back by 30 years. This public debate, sparked by the Singh and Burns (2006) article, led to the Mental Health Act Commission, in their twelfth biennial report, expressing their support for those who were on the other side of the argument to Singh. The report stated, 'We share the concerns of McKenzie.' (Mental Health Act Commission 2008, p.144), referring to an article by McKenzie and Bhui (2007) which had refuted the assertion that charges of racism were unsubstantiated and probably unfounded.

The extent to which mental health services are able to make a difference

Organisations and individuals are hampered by uncertainty about the effectiveness of approaches and interventions or, simply put, 'what works'.

Confidence in the effectiveness of an approach or intervention is important in determining how to prioritise the use of resources. An organisation or individual is more likely to commit time, money and other resources to bring about improvement if they are convinced that their actions will achieve results. Cost-effectiveness is increasingly a consideration in public services (Audit Commission 2006). Organisations make decisions on the ability to achieve the greatest return for the least amount of investment. These decisions at the strategic level within organisations affect the culture and the freedom of staff on the front line. This determines whether they have the knowledge, time, skills or support to be able to invest in working with people from BME groups to achieve a change in trends (Bhui 2002).

That they have a responsibility to do so

Staff in mental health services are sometimes unsure whether they have a responsibility to try to remove or reduce disparities in experience and outcome for different ethnic groups. These disparities may be manifested in over-representation or under-representation in services. If the Chinese community is largely absent in service uptake figures but represented in the local population is it the job of mental health services to try to promote service utilisation? Is it the job of mental health organisations to try to change the consequences of African Caribbean young men having propor- tionally poorer educational outcomes and socio-economic status which is believed to be manifested in more use of their services (Cooper *et al.* 2008)? The national policy Delivering Race Equality makes it clear that the response to these types of questions is yes.

Front-line workers are often set a range of tasks that they feel are unachievable (Evans *et al.* 2006). In practice they perform in a way consis- tent with the adage 'what gets measured (monitored) gets done'. Depending on the ideological viewpoint of workers, there may be a conflict between the limits of what they are able to do and what they would like to do.

The relatively low prioritisation of taking ERC into account arises from a lack of clarity about why it is essential. Research has failed to enable con- sensus to be achieved about the role that ethnicity, race, culture, racial identity and ethnic identity play in patterns of mental health service utilisa- tion. These issues contribute to differences in the pathways into services, the way that services are provided and the service user experience. There is strong evidence that each of these factors have an impact on the relationship between services and BME service users and that these lead to poorer outcomes (Cooper *et al.* 2006). The absence of a detailed understanding of precisely why there are differences according to ERC leads to an absence of a response, or a partial one.

The implication of variations: Ethnicity, race and culture in mental health

Several writers and researchers have attempted to summarise the differences in experience and outcome for people from BME backgrounds (e.g. Bhui

2002; Fernando 1995; Keating 2003). These works draw on a wide range of quantitative research and surveys, analysis of data and qualitative studies. Two aspects are given attention: the *nature of the differences* and the *causes of the differences*. Studies are consistent in suggesting the areas in mental health provision where differences between BME and white British groups are pronounced. The audits of community and inpatient services undertaken by national inspectorate bodies establish datasets about variations. Findings are set out in Commission for Healthcare Audit and Inspection (2007a); Mental Health Act Commission (2006) and Raleigh *et al*. 2007. The information provided includes both quantitative and qualitative findings. Proportionately people from BME backgrounds:

- have more admissions via the criminal justice system

- are over-represented in secure services

- are admitted more frequently under sections of the Mental Health Act

- are placed in seclusion more frequently

- have less utilisation of talking therapies

- feel that they are prescribed higher doses of medication

- express greater dissatisfaction with services

- use community services in significantly disproportionately high numbers.

These findings reflect the overviews of research provided by Bhui (2002); Fernando (1995) and Keating *et al*. (2003). The nature and extent of differences between BME and white groups varies depending on the study. The 2007 *Count Me In* national census of psychiatric inpatients identified as a 'key finding' that various black groups were at least three times more likely (than the average) to be admitted. The 'black other' group was over ten times more likely to be admitted. Black groups and people of black mixed heritage had detention rates (as opposed to informal admissions) between 19 per cent and 38 per cent higher than the average. For admission via the criminal justice system 'white/Asian mixed' were 86 per cent higher than the average; black groups ranged from 33 per cent to 56 per cent higher than average. White/ black Caribbean groups were 33 per cent more likely than the average to be admitted via the criminal justice system (Commission for Healthcare Audit and Inspection 2007a). A detailed set of statistics are now readily available in the annual *Count Me In* Census reports. The disparities identified here are those acknowledged by the report authors to be amongst the areas of most concern.

As stated in Chapter 1, it is erroneous to group together all people from minority backgrounds. There are trends and patterns that relate to specific groups and an understanding of these will have an impact on the type of response offered. Most prominently featured in studies on race and mental health in the UK are the African and African Caribbean groups, primarily because of their over-representation in the high-intervention end of services and the social and psychological impact of this on the service users and their communities as well as the impact on people commissioning or providing services. Recent focus has also been on the economic impact. The policy paper by Sainsbury Centre for Mental Health on the cost of race inequality showed that the excess cost in London of providing services disproportionately to African and African Caribbean people amounts to over £100 million. This is the revenue stream of a small mental health trust (Sainsbury Centre for Mental Health 2006).

Notwithstanding the pronounced variations in relation to black African and African Caribbean people, there are important differences for other groups. Commission for Healthcare Audit and Inspection (2007a); Mental Health Act Commission (2006) and Raleigh *et al.* (2007) show variations for other groups. These groups include people with the following backgrounds:

- Indian subcontinent
- Irish
- mixed heritage
- South East Asian.

Some groups show under-representation in all aspects of service utilisation whereas people from mixed heritage and Irish backgrounds show patterns of variation similar to the black African and black African Caribbean group.

Hypotheses about causes of variations

Many hypotheses have been presented for why the variations exist. Some ideas include a combination of various elements. The main types of argument are:

- biogenetic differences that lead to greater levels of mental illnesses (e.g. Cartwright 1851 quoted in Fernando 1991; Harrison *et al.* 1988)

- cultural factors (e.g. Bhugra and Bhui 2001)
- racist practices, either actively or through passivity in the face of urgent need (e.g. Fernando 1995)
- ignorance or incompetence (e.g. Bowl 2007a)
- socio-economic antecedents, including the impact of racism (e.g. Cooper *et al.* 2008; Trivedi 2002)
- impacts of intergenerational trauma (e.g. Crawford, Nobles and Leary 2003; Davis 2007).

Biogenetic differences

The first documented presentation of this perspective is the diagnosis of drapetamania in slaves who tried to escape. The meaning of this term is the illness of running away. The argument supporting the diagnosis was that a biological illness was driving behaviour (Fernando 1991). Other examples of a 'biological predisposition' explanation of rates of mental illness include the consequence of maternal influenza in immigrants from the Caribbean affecting the mental health of their children (Bhui 2002; Fernando, Ndegwa and Wilson 1998). Biogenetic arguments are not expressed overtly nowadays as they lead to irrfutable claims of racism.

Cultural factors

It had been a common argument that cultural misunderstanding leads to misdiagnoses but this is used less frequently as an explanation. Religion, faith and spirituality are covered within this heading. Much is written about different cultural presentations of mental health problems (Littlewood and Lipsedge 1989; Rack 1982). Less is written about culture as a single variable in potential causes of differences in experience and outcome in mental health services. Culture is associated with other forms of difference, e.g. physical presentation (dress), language and religion.

Racist practices

This line of analysis leads to strong reactions and is perhaps the most polarising of arguments. Minnis *et al.* (2001) report on a survey that elicited racial stereotyping by psychiatrists. Fernando (1991) McKenzie and Bhui (2007) and Bhui (2002) advocate accepting the explanation that various forms of racism are the cause of the different experiences and outcomes for BME groups whilst Singh and Burns (2006) directly opposes the global application of this argument. Arguments about racism in mental health generate newspaper headlines and embroil senior politicians in these (*Guardian* 2005). This occurred around the launch of the government's response to the recommendations of the inquiry into the care and treatment of a black patient, Rocky Bennett, who died whilst being restrained by nurses on a psychiatric ward (NSCSTHA 2003). There is often a lack of understanding about the difference between individuals being racist and institutional racism. Racism is still often associated with the behaviour of extreme groups and not, for example, the passive observance of inequality with an insufficient response, either in scope or urgency (McKenzie and Bhui 2007). Some people argue that the focus on racism is unhelpful as it undermines people doing difficult jobs but failure to define the problem accurately weakens the proposed solution, as discussed in Chapter 1. The reluctance to accept racism as an explanation stems in part from an unwillingness to recognise acts of stereotyping. Those attributes that may be regarded by the critical mind as being racist stereotypes are held by mainstream society as common-sense descriptions of types of persons. As Banton (1967, p.58) states, 'race is a role sign only in multiracial societies or in situations of racial contact in which expectations of behaviour have become crystallized into patterns of some sort'.

Ignorance or incompetence

Alternative explanations for variations in experiences and outcomes for BME groups are that problems arise because of ignorance and incompetence although these explanations seek to avoid being judgemental. This is captured well in the MacPherson (1999) definition of institutional racism given in Chapter 1 which refers to acts that are 'unwitting'. This reference makes the point that the individual unwitting acts lead to a collective failure that amounts to racism. Examples of unwitting acts include assuming that a black person will not have a higher education qualification or that an Asian service user will be supported by a strong extended family. The lower proportion of people from BME backgrounds referred for talking therapies is a prime example of this analysis (Raleigh *et al.* 2007).

Socio-economic antecedents

This is one of the main paradigms used in analysing the causes of the patterns of service utilisation by BME groups. It covers the negative impact of disadvantage in relation to education, safeguarding children (child protection), the criminal justice system, housing, employment, racist attacks (verbal and physical) and poverty. Morgan *et al.* (2005a) and Cooper *et al.* (2008) highlight the likely connection between these factors and poor mental health even prior to entering the system. This is an acknowledgement that racism and disadvantage has a negative impact on mental health but does not attempt to explain it beyond the contribution to stress. This does not suggest that all those arguing these theories believe that stress on its own causes serious mental health problems. Many argue, however, that society is certainly toxic for people from BME groups and African and Caribbean people in particular (Bhui 2002; Cooper *et al.* 2008; Fernando 1995; Jones, Cross and DeFour 2007; Morgan *et al.* 2005a; Singh *et al.* 2007).

Impacts of intergenerational trauma

As understanding grows in psychotherapy about the impact of intergenerational trauma arising from abuse this learning is applied to historical events such as slavery (Arnold 2007; Crawford *et al.* 2003; Davis 2007). Intergenerational trauma is seen in families of holocaust victims (Wiseman, Metzl and Barber 2006). This paradigm offers an explanation for why African and African Caribbean people in particular have poor outcomes and experience across virtually every measure of wellbeing.

Though there is less knowledge or understanding of these arguments there is something persuasive about this idea. It has a clear evidence base, and it offers some explanation for the wide-ranging poor experiences. Fanon (1967) explored these issues and provides a foundation for current thinking on this. This subject is developed further in Chapter 9.

Toxic Interactions Theory – a new perspective

Arguments can become polarised so that either services and society are seen as causing poorer mental health in some groups or the groups are culpable either because of a deficiency in their biology / genetics, culture or lifestyle. The landmark *Breaking the Circles of Fear* (Sainsbury Centre for Mental Health 2002a) presented a way of thinking about the dynamic being two-directional. The underlying message remained that services, through their inadequacies, fuel poor reactions in African and African Caribbean people and communities.

An extension of this concept is the 'Toxic Interactions Theory'. The fundamental thrust of this theory is that it is the mixing of certain elements that creates the problem rather than solely the attributes or behaviour of one or other party. Scrutiny of BME groups (either biology or culture) will not lead to the most compelling explanation nor will a single focus on the behaviours of society – and of mental health services in particular (Veling *et al.* 2007).

'Interactions' are described as potential causes of poorer outcome, dissatisfaction or incidence of mental health problems in various studies

(McLean, Campbell and Cornish 2003; Sainsbury Centre for Mental Health 2002a; Singh *et al.* 2007).

McLean *et al.* (2003, p.667) discuss social exclusion as 'a framework to understand interactions between the African Caribbean Community and the health service'. The Sainsbury Centre for Mental Health Report (2002a, p.29) states that 'It is clear that these fears impact negatively on the interactions between Black people and mental health services.' Singh *et al.* (2007, p.102) – cites, amongst others, 'patient–service interaction' as an explanation for disparities.

The toxic effect of society on BME groups is described in Bhui (2002), Fernando (1991) in the UK and Veling *et al.* (2007) in the Netherlands. The US study by Jones *et al.* 2007 describes 'the toxicity stemming from unfair race-based treatment' (p.209). Further, the Sainsbury Centre for Mental Health report (2002a) states that 'this review shows that mental health services mirror the social relations of Black people with other institutions' (p.68).

BOX 2.1 TOXIC INTERACTIONS THEORY

Toxic Interactions Theory can be described as the damaging effect specific to the collision of the emotions and presentations arising from black people's experiences, with the fears and anxieties of white people. A protective strategy is adopted by black people whereby a strong racial identity is accentuated (Davis 2007; Tizard and Phoenix 1993). This is experienced as threatening blackness by white people, resulting in a determination to deny it or suppress it (Ward 2006). The centrality of race in personal identity increases the potency of racist stress events (Jones *et al.* 2007; Sellers *et al.* 2003). The effect of this interaction is a fracture in psychic architecture for black people (Fanon 1967) and the narcissistic disabling guilt of white people combined with anger (often suppressed) driven by a fear of erosion of their own identity and rights, leading to internal dissonance (Wright 2006).

Toxic Interactions (TI) Theory locates the problem in the interaction rather than the parties involved. Conceptually the toxic interactions occur in the 'carrier' or the crucible of the relationship both on the individual and societal levels. In multicultural societies the crucible cannot be avoided; BME people will not disappear. The only solution is to add something to the mix to neutralise the toxic interactions. Attention must be focused on altering the relationship between black people and white people to reduce its toxicity.

TI Theory explained

For people from BME backgrounds and for white people the colliding of worlds forces difference to the fore (Banton 1967). The greater the difference, the more pronounced the impact, as seen for people of the African Diaspora – black African and Caribbean people (Veling *et al.* 2007).

The accentuation of a strong individual identity may find its outlet in interests or roles that are either socially acceptable or unacceptable. The desire for status and respect as a result of racism does not provoke an equal and opposite reaction. The successful black lawyer and the criminal who can afford fancy cars may both be exhibiting reactions to racism in their own personal choices.

The description of 'fracture of the psychic structure' (as described by Fanon 1967) is the process that occurs when the relationships and constructs in the world that are supposed to provide safety and positive reinforcement are found to be those that attack. He argues that to a black child this equates to relationships with white people in authority and institutions. The psychological defences used appear bizarre if the stimuli are not recognised. Black people, Fanon argues, exhibit trauma reactions as a result of living in racist multiracial societies.

Application to practice

TI Theory requires that all workers in mainstream mental health services would work with service users on the assumption that the relationship is going to be toxic unless something specific is done to neutralise this. There are many levels at which relationships work. White workers who appear to be representing a 'white' system will face a greater challenge than staff from BME groups. The BME workers will however bring into the relationship with black service users an identity as part of the institution. However, there will be a degree of toxicity derived from this fact alone. The Sainsbury Centre for Mental Health report *Breaking the Circles of Fear* (2002a) is clear that some of the reactions described by black service users and families are in relation to the 'institutions' of mental health and not just to white people. The amelioration of the toxic effect needs to be conscious and proactive. Chapter 5 is dedicated to exploring how this may be done.

Toxic Interactions Theory and many of the other explanatory perspectives place a responsibility on services to accept their role in the creation or perpetuation of variations in experiences and outcomes for BME groups. Services are sometimes unclear as to whether any evidence exists for their contribution to the negative experiences and outcomes for people from BME backgrounds. The meta-analysis by Singh *et al.* (2007), however, identifies that the readmission rates for people from BME groups increase over time, indicating that the toxicity of interactions exists within mental health services and not just society as a whole. In an ideal world, organisations would be able to assess mental health at entry and exits points from services and in doing so, measure success. It would then be possible to assess the variations between success rates across ethnic groups. The Sainsbury Centre for Mental Health set out the fundamental problems with trying to measure the results of mental health services in this way in their Policy Paper 4 (Sainsbury Centre for Mental Health 2004). These include the variability of presentations and treatment and response to treatments, and also the often episodic nature of mental health problems. The most telling information about the added value of services over time can be found in analysing the BME utilisation of different aspects of service. Tools such as Health of the Nation Outcome Scales (Wing *et al.* 1998) are used to assess outcomes in terms of recovery from a service user's perspective. Early suggestions from those developing the Pay by Results (PbR) regime in mental health is that Health of the Nation Outcome scales is to be used as a measure for recovery. PbR is the government's mechanism for linking the funding of NH Trusts they deliver and involves agreeing units of measurement and the tariffs associated with these.

Relationships between areas of variation

The mass of statistics and evidence and experience of inequality presents a picture that is disheartening for those trying to make a difference. Without the application of detailed thought and analysis, the data and information does not convey the role of services in contributing to patterns. Each local area will have differences but there are some key relationships between pieces of information, which when considered together provide a clearer picture of the role of services. Services (and individual workers) may achieve one of three possible outcomes:

- improvement in the overall experience and outcome for BME groups

- failure to have any impacts on the poor level of experience and outcomes

- worsen the overall experience and outcome.

One way of assessing this is to understand what can be inferred from the utilisation data from different services. The starting point to this analysis is the acknowledgement of a simple point, i.e. that those responsible for services often argue that the poor experiences and outcomes for BME groups are due their level of need at the point that they enter the mental health system. Put another way, at the point of entry, people from BME backgrounds proportionately have a higher degree of complexity in their needs. Tracking the response to this difference can be done by considering utilisation of services at different stages in the service user care pathway.

Table 2.1 Utilisation of different services

Type of service utilisation	Typical pattern of utilisation by BME groups	What can be inferred
All community services in an NHS Trust combined	Significant over-representation by Irish, African and African Caribbean people Under-representation of Chinese, and Asian from the Indian subcontinent	Over-represented groups a) breach tight thresholds for entry into services and b) come to the attention of services more frequently For under-represented groups the reverse is true
Assertive Outreach (functionalised team, working with more complexity than community mental health teams (CMHTs))	Significant over-representation by Irish, African and African Caribbean people (at least as, or more significant than, the variation in CMHTs) Under-representation of Chinese, and Asian from the Indian Subcontinent	As the criteria include being 'hard to engage' and 'repeat admissions' this indicates that NHS Trusts have not achieved an impact on poorer trends despite the knowledge that there is a greater level of need
Admissions under section 3 of the Mental Health Act 1983	African Caribbean and Irish people are over-represented	Typically people admitted under section 3 are known to services. This means that workers are more effective in working with white British service users to prevent breakdowns than they are Irish and African/African Caribbean people
Repeat admissions	African, African Caribbean and Irish people are over-represented	By definition, these are people known to services. This means that workers are more effective in working with white British service users to prevent breakdowns than they are Irish and African/African Caribbean people

Use of seclusion	African, African Caribbean and Irish people are over-represented	Staff have not been able to do anything different to prevent the realisation of the known risk that these groups will be disproportionately subjected to seclusion

Commission for Healthcare Audit and Inspection (2007a); Mental Health Act Commission (2006); Raleigh *et al.* (2007)

The choice of service utilisation considered in Table 2.1 relates to those aspects of provision that are the mainstay of statutory mental health services. They are aspects that demonstrate that the input of services has failed to make an impact on adverse patterns. Reasonable questions for any provider to answer are given in Box 2.2.

BOX 2.2 SERVICE UTILISATION: KEY QUESTIONS

- Given that there are known risks that certain BME groups will have poorer experiences and outcomes, what have been the specific inputs on the service user care pathway to alleviate these risks?

And further:

- How have these inputs changed the variations at different stages of the pathway?

These questions are equally relevant to the corporate organisation and to every individual front-line worker.

Taking ethnicity, race and culture into account as a practitioner

From a practitioner's point of view, service utilisation statistics indicate one major point; if no specific steps are taken to prevent negative patterns (inequality) the default position is likely to be continued inequality. This is corroborated by virtually every piece of research into the subject.

Failure to attempt to mitigate the risk of racial inequality amounts to racial discrimination. With this in mind it is fair to say that unless every practitioner considers ERC (and responds robustly) they are potentially, through their lack of action, perpetuating negative patterns. But as Bhui (2002, p.223) states, 'as a society and as organisations we lack the capacity to talk about race and culture'.

It is perhaps unsurprising that mental health professionals experience fears and anxieties despite their specific training and supervision. There are a number of reasons why this is the case.

Examples of why this is so are listed in Box 2.3.

BOX 2.3 COMPLICATIONS PRACTITIONERS FACE IN TAKING ACCOUNT OF ETHNICITY, RACE AND CULTURE

Practitioners who *do* raise race, ethnicity and culture, particularly when working with someone of a different background may:

- fear getting it wrong
- worry that they will be seen as viewing the service user narrowly through the lens of race
- worry that they will be viewed as over-compensating for racist feelings
- fear that they may end up being a trigger for making race an issue when it wasn't one
- worry about a white backlash if their engagement with race leads to tailored (or 'special') provision for BME service users.

Practitioners who *do not* delve into race, ethnicity and culture may:

- feel ill-equipped
- defer to specialist 'black' services
- take the lead from an organisation that they experience as colour blind or offering lip-service to the subject
- feel that there are no services available to meet the needs that they may identify
- feel they have too many demands on their time to engage in deep explorations, meaning that their relationship with the service user needs to be primarily functional
- deny that ethnicity or race or culture matters, other than the way that the service user presents, i.e. any problems that arise are to do with the service user and not the practitioner or the service.

(Ahmad 1990; Dominelli 1992; Fernando et al. 1998)

Mental health practitioners find themselves in a position where they have to make a simple choice; confront and deal with the barriers to effective work or remain passive and, in so doing, become complicit in the perpetuation of racial inequality.

Overcoming personal fears

BOX 2.4 EXAMPLE

Fredrick is deputy manager in Jules Meadow, a third-sector day service. The purpose of the service is 'to enable service users to make a process of recovery, through offering and facilitating access to meaningful daytime activity'. Fredrick is aware that once Jules Meadow accepts a referral, care coordinators from the community mental health team (CMHT) reduce their input into the care plan to negligible levels. A consequence of this is that when service users begin to feel in crisis Jules Meadow has to alert the CMHT and invite them to increase their level of involvement. Fredrick noticed in his three years working at Jules Meadow that service users from BME backgrounds appeared to have more frequent readmission than white service users. He felt that he and his colleagues did the same type of work with all the day service users and did not feel that they did anything to contribute to the difference in outcome. He also realised that although he and his colleagues were aware from research that people from BME backgrounds had poorer outcomes they worked uniformly with all service users.

In his next supervision with the manager of Jules Meadow, Fredrick discussed his observation and after joint reflection agreed that he would offer a specific and enhanced service for African Caribbean people to help improve their engagement.

Two months later in supervision Suzzie, Fredrick's manager, noted that though he had seemed enthused in their conversation, he has not returned with plans to implement what they had agreed. Fredrick explained his dilemma. He had floated the idea of setting up a black service user group to work on strategies for anticipating and presenting breakdowns but colleagues had raised various objections. These included claims that it was divisive and that other groups were just as in need of such a group.

Fredrick considered whether he could offer more one-to-one time with black service users but calculated that this would just put more pressure on his already stretched time.

Behind Fredrick's reticence was his nervousness in relation to speaking about race, ethnicity and culture as a means of reducing disparities. He was conscious that this would mark a departure from previous practice. He was worried that service users from BME backgrounds would be sceptical and that his approach would be inadequate.

Fredrick realised that he was treating the subject as if it were something personal when in fact it was a measure of his own practice. He asked himself three questions:

- What might I do if there was another aspect of my performance where I was failing to achieve targets?
- What information can I use in conversations with service users to illustrate the reasons for the new focus on these issues?
- How might I use the relationship with service users as a medium for change?

In working through these questions Fredrick concluded that:

- He had a clear sense of the inputs required to improve outcomes for other aspects of his work. He needed to be equally clear about this in relation to working with BME groups
- There were reports emerging throughout his annual work cycle that would legitimately trigger a focus on steps to redress disparities. These included the results of service user surveys, complaints reports, inpatient census for the local NHS Trust and general performance reports. He decided to look at the findings of the surveys, census and other reports and to use the key messages regarding disparities to open conversations. For example, Fredrick referred to the findings of the inpatient census. This included information that a disproportionate number of black people were inpatients and were subjected to seclusion. He started conversations with: 'I've just seen a study that tells us that …' or 'I'm not sure what you feel about it but evidence suggests that race/ethnicity/culture makes a big difference in what happens in mental health services. Usually for people of a BME background this isn't positive. I'm hoping together you and I can do something to turn the tide.'

Fredrick built on the last sentence ('I'm hoping together you and I can do something to turn the tide') and located possibilities for change in the relationship with BME service users. He made race and racism explicit points of reference, using language such as 'we' and 'together'. Fredrick handled his anxiety by acknowledging with service users that inaction in the face of inequality was hard to defend.

All workers will have different personal styles, local contexts and fears and anxieties. It is important that the approach used by Fredrick is adapted so that each worker feels that it is meaningful to his or her situation. The exercise that follows is designed to assist in this process.

BOX 2.5 EXERCISE

List five ways in which you take ERC into account your work.
What areas of probable inequality in the lives of service users from BME groups are you trying to ameliorate or mitigate against in your actions?
What prevents you from doing more, in terms of:

- your own beliefs about the responsibility, culpability or rights of BME groups
- your own fears about reactions from BME service users or from colleagues
- limits in the support from your organisation in terms of time (capacity), education, learning and development and access to specialist services?

For these last three points create a table with two columns, headed 'obstacles' and 'actions to overcome these'. List the three points above in the left-hand column, then write down your personal action plan for overcoming these barriers.

Conclusion

The evidence is overwhelmingly convincing that mental health services in a multiracial, multiethnic society need to pay attention to ERC and mitigate against the risks of adverse experiences and outcomes. Modern mental health services are driven by risk assessment and management. It is unfortunate that these principles are not applied to a group of people who have a disproportionate risk of having poor outcomes. There is a need for targeted and differentiated approaches to manage the increased risks to people from BME backgrounds.

CHAPTER 3

QUALITY ASSESSMENTS

The assessment process for mental health users is complex and particular issues arise specifically in relation to people from BME backgrounds. This chapter will explore the nature of an assessment. It will consider that an assessment comprises of a number of activities; the potential for the process to be ongoing; and the role of the practitioner or service in it. The role of risk will be considered, as will the difference between person-centred and service-led approaches. Practitioners will be encouraged to analyse the components of an assessment and to develop a critical perspective. Suggestions are made for practical measures that can be taken to ameliorate the potentially negative effects of information that is contributed to the assessment process.

The term 'assessment' describes a collection of activities undertaken and usually documented, to ensure a response to need. 'Assessment is a process not an event' (Davis, Bebbington and Charnley 1990, p.317). This principle is important for two reasons. First, an assessment is not just a precursor to the development of a care or treatment plan, ending at a point when that care or treatment commences. Second, an assessment is not an exercise in completing documentation and, as such, not purely an act of gathering information that has been specifically requested (e.g. on an assessment form) (Baldwin 1997; Trevithick 2005).

These points are often obscured in the parlance of modern mental health services where assessments are referred to as objects (e.g. sending an 'assessment'). Routinely practitioners describe an activity as 'undertaking an assessment' as opposed to 'undertaking an interview as part of the assessment process'. It is customary in all fields for shorthand language or jargon to develop. It is important, however, that reductive language does not lead to reductive thinking or practice.

Components of an assessment

Literature is consistent in presenting some common components of robust assessments:

- communicating with the service user and gathering information from what is said and from behaviour

- gathering information from existing records

- gathering information from other agencies

- gathering information from significant others such as family and friends

- weighing up the relative accuracy and reliability of information.

(Baldwin 1997; Davis *et al.* 1990;
Social Care Institute for Excellence 2003; Trevithick 2005)

In health and social care settings the assessment is influenced by an under-standing of what may be offered to meet the assessed needs (Davis *et al.* 1990). 'Person-centred assessments' distinguished from service-led assess-ments. The latter are based on seeing needs from the perspective of the services available or from real or perceived responsibilities of the service, such as protecting the public. For example, some assessments refer to a service user as being in need of a day-centre place whereas in reality this is shorthand for a range of considerations, such as a need for social contact or perhaps undertaking a specific activity. Failure to define the need more pre-cisely perpetuates the reliance on established services and structures (San-derson, Thompson and Kilbane 2006). Person-led assessments take more account of what service users consider as their needs. Practitioners may con-tribute and encourage the consideration of a broader range of possibilities than those suggested by the service user. The aim is to achieve a partnership with the emphasis remaining on the individual's definition of what he or she needs.

An assessment of need is usually underpinned by an assessment of risk. The assessment will consider risk to the individual and to others. This is complex because the risk assessment can include a wide range of aspects, for example risks arising from individuals' own actions in relation to them-selves and others and the risks to them from the actions of other people.

It is the risk assessment of the service user's behaviour in relation to other people that often features most saliently in relation to black people in mental health services (Desai 2006; Fernando *et al.* 1998). This is captured excellently in the *Breaking the Circles of Fear* report (Sainsbury Centre for

Mental Health 2002a). The authors argue that a cycle develops where black people are reticent about using services and enter in crisis more frequently (with the potential for behaviour perceived as being threatening). This, the authors say, leads to a perception within services that black people are more threatening and a resultant culture and practice develops that is more coercive and controlling in relation to this group. This has the effect of creating a fear in black people about the type of experience that they or their loved ones will receive, leading to further reluctance about contacting services and delay, by which point their presentation is acute, fulfilling the expectation of services.

This summary of the *Breaking the Circles of Fear* report highlights an important point that this chapter will go on to explore further. The process of undertaking an assessment is not a neutral act. The person undertaking the assessment brings something of him- or herself to the process and the outcome.

Ethnicity, race and culture and the assessment process

The process of assessment is clearly complex. For practitioners to improve their practice in relation to people from BME backgrounds the relationships between ERC and the component parts of an assessment need to be understood.

Returning to the elements of the assessment process set out earlier, and the influences upon them, the following issues will be considered:

- information gathered from what the service user communicates verbally and non-verbally
- third-party information
    - the referral itself
    - gathering information from existing records
    - gathering information from other agencies
- gathering information from significant others such as family and friends
- weighing up the relative accuracy and reliability of information
- the role of the practitioner in the assessment
- the impact of the organisation's culture and predominant practice.

Information gathered from the service user

The voice of the service user is often not given its due prominence. Behaviours, rich as a source of information, are often narrowly interpreted. A worker may interpret that a service user poses a risk to him- or herself or others but patterns or themes in breakdowns may go unobserved. Service users are not asked to explain. 'It is sometimes argued about mental heath teams that the voice of the client may be lost in the clamour of professionals claiming to speak with client insight' (Davis *et al.* 1990, p.319). Service users often have important contributions to make to their risk assessments (Langan and Lindow 2004). Male service users from African Caribbean backgrounds (who represent those with the greatest disparities in mental health services) express many concerns about their voices not being heard. Advocacy is seen as part of the solution to getting their voices heard and for change to occur (Newbigging *et al.* 2008).

Third-party Information

A referral indicates that someone feels that something needs to be done about a problem. It indicates that this is beyond the capability or the remit of the referrer. It is typical for referrers to mental health services to give their indication as to what needs to be done. The content of the referral is influenced by the referrer's view of what needs to be done. The assessment has therefore partly begun by the time the practitioner receiving the referral actually begins his or her work.

ERC has an impact on how people refer. For people from BME backgrounds this is often negative. There is not consensus amongst researchers about whether there is an increased perception of risk in relation to people from certain BME groups (Dein, Williams and Dein 2007). Fernando *et al* 1998, however, having reviewed various studies, conclude that referrals in relation to black people are more likely to present perceptions of threatening behaviour. With this possibility in mind it is important for practitioners to analyse referrals critically. Referrals should be analysed from the perspective that it is *probable* that race has had a negative impact on the content of the referral but it should not be assumed that this is necessarily the case. It is improbable that race routinely has a neutral or positive influence (Bhui and Sashidharan 2003; Fernando *et al.* 1998).

Gathering information from significant others such as family and friends

Carers, families and friends are often seen by the systems as allies in their function of preserving social control or they are seen as obstacles to the service achieving its plans (Fernando 2005). Some stereotypes of BME families (i.e. that they 'stick together') lead to insufficient exploration of competing wishes from the service user and carer perspectives (Keating *et al.* 2003). An alternative challenge is the potential for loved ones to be seen as another element of the problems that come with providing care and treatment to people from BME backgrounds. This may relate to the passion with which the family/carer advocates on behalf of the service user, an accent (or level of spoken English) that the practitioner finds difficult to understand or a belief that they are colluding with the service user in non-compliance.

Weighing up the accuracy and reliability of information

In analysing the referral it is important to consider why certain information has been included in the referral, what has been emphasised and what has been excluded. It will be beneficial to apply knowledge of previous findings about how people from BME backgrounds are viewed. An attempt should be made to explore whether information from another perspective could have been included in the referral.

Table 3.1 sets out potential content of referrals specifically for black people. This group is considered separately because there are significant differences in the content of referrals according to ethnic group. The column 'Potential questions' provides examples of the types of questions that may be posed when considering the content of a referral. Table 3.2 considers information presented in relation to other minority ethnic groups.

Table 3.1 Critical analysis of referrals for black people

Content of referral	What evidence tells us	Potential questions
Concerned due to levels of arousal	Black people are often considered as more dangerous (Desai 2006; Fernando *et al.* 1998) Evidence has indicated that black people come to the attention of services at a later stage and therefore are more acute in their presentations (Bhui *et al.* 2003). However research from Mohan *et al.* (2006) and Morgan *et al.* (2005b) contrasts with previous findings	Are there contexts in which the person's behaviour is considered as 'less bizarre'? What are the triggers? What support had the person received before coming to the attention of services? Have potential solutions been sought outside of statutory services? What details have been provided to corroborate the concern about the level of arousal?

Content of referral	What evidence tells us	Potential questions
Violent / threatening	Evidence illustrates that violence in black people (men in particular) is expected and is therefore more likely to be identified as a risk (Dein *et al*. 2007)	What has been explored with the service user about triggers, or his or her view of underlying cause?
Poor impulse control	Black people are more likely to be seen as unpredictable and volatile (Fernando *et al*. 1998)	What evidence exists that effort has been made to give attention to the root cause? What specific information has been provided to corroborate statements?
Angry	Black people are less satisfied with services and are angry about what they perceive as unfair treatment (Sainsbury Centre for Mental Health 2002)	As above. What reasons have been given by the service user for why he or she is angry?
Not keen on talking therapies	Black people identify the lack of talking treatments high on their list of causes for dissatisfaction with services (Wilson 1993). Black people are less frequently referred to therapy (McKenzie *et al*. 2001)	Have different approaches been considered, such as alternatives to Western psychological therapies?
Has a chip on his or her shoulder Paranoid.	Race and the experience of racism features far more prominently than many clinicians acknowledge (Karlsen *et al*. 2005)	What are the examples of racism that the service user would regard as having shaped his or her outlook? What has been the specific impact?

The comments in the first coloumn are just examples of many that appear in referrals and previous records.

Existing records may be several inches thick or just a few pages. When reviewing very long files it will be important to seek out information that supports a different perspective to the predominant one in the records. For example, early records may detail the context of any violence or may include accounts of racism or abuse, which are subsequently omitted from reports in favour of a simple, almost one-dimensional portrayal of an individual.

OTHER MINORITY ETHNIC GROUPS

Black groups feature most frequently in research and literature. There is logic in the intent to try to close the inequality gap where it is greatest. Studies indicate that African and African Caribbean groups experience the greatest degree of inequality, though the Commission for Healthcare Audit and Inspection (2007a) identifies variations for other groups. These include proportionally higher rates of disparities for the 'Black other' groups and large variations for the 'Asian other' group although these are for smaller numbers of people. Raleigh *et al.* (2007) identify some more variations in community services relating to Asian groups such as reports of lack of services.

Third-party information often includes oblique stereotypical references about Asian and other minority ethnic groups. Examples of the evidence and potential challenges are shown in Table 3.2.

The impact of the practitioner on the assessment

It is important that practitioners consider how their beliefs, attitudes and practice have an impact on the assessment (Bhugra and Bhui 2001). As Bhui and Sashidharan (2003, p.10) state 'professionals are still not equipped with conceptual skills and knowledge to offer equity in assessment'.

Thomas (1992) uses concepts from psychotherapy to present the phenomenon whereby there is an assumed knowledge of the black service user before the first meeting occurs. He makes the distinction between this (described as pre-transference by Andrew Curry (1964)) and stereotyping, which happens contemporaneously. A problem is created by 'pre-transference' whereby white workers need to mentally displace the person they have constructed to engage with the real person with whom they will work. Bhui and Sashidharan (2003, p.10) state that 'perceived differences between racial and ethnic groups conjure up much racial imagery that is unconsciously introduced into social encounters'.

The impact of the organisation's culture and predominant practice

Practitioners must anticipate that there are many factors that create a *default position*, that is, a shared common-sense belief about certain BME groups, which means that stereotyping goes unnoticed. The conclusion to be drawn from the concept of the default position is that unless specific steps are taken to counter these perceptions and working assumptions the system works on the basis that these are true. Fanon (1967) utilises Carl Jung's concept of the

**Table 3.2 Critical analysis of referrals for
Asian and other minority ethnic groups**

Content of referral	What evidence tells us	Potential questions
Complex (large) family with lots of links back home	Many BME communities have networks of support from family and friends and have approaches that do not focus on people as individuals but as part of a larger social or family unit (Bhugra and Bhui 2001). Services are poor at engaging them Services often assume family support, uncritically. Service providers do not fulfil their obligations based on a belief that families will provide help (Keating *et al.* 2003)	Is there evidence in current records of any discussion with the service user and his or her family (where appropriate) about the family taking on a 'carer' role? Has this been explored explicitly?
Not very keen to have input from 'outside'	'Many studies suggest that irrespective of ethnicity, people will turn to their natural support systems first' (Bhugra, Lippett and Cole 1999, p.36)	Do the family members have the confidence of the service user? What are the specific issues being raised by the family?
Service user appears to be experiencing a conflict arising from differences between cultures/generations	There are sometimes intergenerational conflicts but it is the fact that this operates in a context of perceived external scrutiny by the white majority that makes it more problematic (Sewell 2004). Some groups consider that services avoid their issues because, cultural rather than language misunderstanding frustrate them (Green *et al.* 2002). Many people described as 'second generation' BME are competently bi-cultural (Bhugra and Bhui *et al.* 2001).	Who makes this point? Is this a convenient explanation offered by professionals or family members? How does the service user understand his or her problems?
Service user does not speak English but family members will happily interpret	Service users feel dissatisfied with the reliance on family members to interpret (Bowl 2007a; Green *et al.* 2002)	Is there evidence that the individual is not understood fully? What are the consequences of this? Is there evidence that professional interpretation has been offered?

collective unconscious in explaining this. If a group or community share common beliefs, transactions are able to take place based on what is inferred and correctly interpreted, avoiding the need for direct reference to these beliefs. This establishes and reinforces cultural norms.

BOX 3.1 ILLUSTRATION

An example can be taken from the author's direct experience. An Approved Social Worker (ASW) was advised by a consultant psychiatrist that police 'back-up' would be required for a Mental Health Act assessment because the (black, male) client had a history of violence. This information had been passed from a nurse. When asked for details of the incidents of violence and what precipitated these, the consultant psychiatrist was unable to provide background information. Though the ASW would check file records before undertaking the MHA assessment it was evident that comments had taken on a sense of truth because of the shared view amongst the professionals in the team that young black men are more likely to be violent.

The important point in this example was not whether or not the person being referred had been violent in the past but that there appeared to be an acceptance of a powerful and potentially damning piece of information without its validity being tested.

The challenge to practitioners is to ensure that their practice does not contribute to a compounding of stereotypes and assumptions. It is important that full and accurate information is taken into account in assessments and passed on as necessary. It is equally important for information to be verified and for this to be balanced and contextualised. The concept of the *prejudicial default position* places a responsibility on practitioners. This term refers to the behaviours and outcomes that will occur most naturally in the absence of critical thought or challenge Practitioners need to be mindful of this default and interrogate their own beliefs, practices and assumptions, as well as those of others. As Fernando (1991, p.143) put it, 'to ignore race is racist'.

Racism Diagnostic and Review Tool (RaDAR Tool)

The potential for racism to permeate the assessment processes requires that there should be mechanisms in place to test whether this is occurring. The Race Relations (Amendment) Act (2000) requires public bodies to undertake race equality impact assessments (REIAs) to assess whether policies or functions have an unfair impact on certain minority ethnic groups, and to address any potential differences. Organisations now tend to implement single equality impact assessments (covering at least race, gender and disability) following the introduction of the Disability Discrimination Act 2005 and the Equalities Act 2006, but they have their genesis in REIAs.

The principles of REIAs can be applied to front-line practice. There are two key stages in undertaking REIAs. The screening stage assesses whether there is likely to be a differential impact, prompting a detailed assessment. The key elements of the assessment stage of a REIA are identifying:

- trends of service uptake

- what research and studies have indicated about differences on the basis of race

- the impact of any policy or function

- the community or customer (service user) feedback or views.

At the level of individual practice the process is similar. There should be a constant process of checking whether racism is affecting processes and outcomes. This racism need not be considered as an evil act perpetrated by individuals but could be the institutional racism discussed in Chapter 1 and the inadvertent practices referred to earlier as the *prejudicial default position*. A useful tool for practitioners, the Racism Diagnostic and Review Tool (RaDAR Tool), has been developed as a synthesis of the ideas and processes of questioning used in Tables 3.1 and 3.2.

An essential aspect of professional practice is self-evaluation. Much work happens in one-to-one relationships with service users. Even group work or practice in environments such as residential or day services relies on some level of individual practitioner interaction with service users. Feedback from a colleague or service user may prompt reflection and self-evaluation but this should not be the only ways by which change is achieved. Supervision is critical in promoting reflection and improvements in practice, though the content of supervision is usually based on secondary information. Beyond education and development (e.g. practice placements) very little practice is observed and evaluated. Self-evaluation underpins professional practice and is a dynamic process that occurs on an ongoing basis.

Self-evaluation around ERC can often be difficult because the emotive nature of the subject affects the ability of workers to be honest with themselves. Few if any practitioners in mental health services would be comfortable in assessing their own performance as being discriminatory or racist. As Bhui and Sashidharan (2003, p.10) state, 'no one in the caring professions wishes detrimental treatment on any member of the public, irrespective of cultural origins'. There is a disincentive to identifying poor practice because the outcome would be for practitioners to feel not only that their practice was bad but that they themselves were bad. This is an impact of the loaded nature of racial discrimination. It is essential, therefore, for practitioners to have a tool that enables them to review their own practice based on a critical evaluation and not just on their feelings. Thomas (1992, p.134) makes the point, 'it is extremely difficult for any form of racism, accrued from a lifetime of socialisation, to be brought to personal awareness, yet this is indeed what needs to take place'.

The RaDAR Tool presented below provides a simple way for practitioners to assess the extent to which their own practice contributes to poorer outcomes for people from BME backgrounds. Based on the MacPherson (1999) definition (see Chapter 1), institutional racism is considered to be at work where outcomes are poorer for BME groups and where practices, however unwitting they are, contribute to these. The ability of individual practitioners to evaluate their own role in the process is important because institutional racism arises from the collective impact of behaviours. Mental health practitioners whose practice contributes to poorer outcomes for BME groups may be working in a way that is consistent with their organisation's culture or policies but in absolute terms they are contributors to institutional racism. This is particularly the case where there is prior knowledge of disparities based on race but no action has been taken to mitigate these risks.

BOX 3.2 RADAR

RaDAR asks:
Do I know whether people on my caseload from BME backgrounds have poorer experiences of working with me and my service?

Do I know whether BME people on my caseload have poorer outcomes in relation to:
- self-defined recovery
- experience of restrictions, such as detentions under the Mental Health Act 1983, locked wards or seclusion
- repeat admissions?

Do I utilise information available such as findings from the national service user survey, inpatient census, local service user feedback?

Do I know how my own professional practice may have a differential impact according to ethnic background?

What steps have I taken in relation to the evidence that suggests that unless specific action is taken to prevent poorer outcomes for people from BME backgrounds, this is likely to occur?

These questions will help to highlight areas for potential improvement in a practitioner's drive to tackle the long-standing negative trends in BME service user outcomes. Unless workers individually improve, the collective impact will remain negative, no matter how unwittingly this occurs.

Conclusion

Assessments include different components, each of which is susceptible to the influences of race. Uncritical utilisation of information gathered in the assessment process can lead to the perpetuation of stereotypes. A lack of challenge can contribute to institutional racism. Practitioners are encouraged to apply their expertise in risk assessment to considering the increased risks of poorer outcomes to people from BME backgrounds. The findings from research studies indicate that there are certain default positions – the natural trend – that will be maintained unless something is done specifically to try to counter these.

The assessment determines how need is considered and therefore the nature of the service response. The process of the assessment is influenced by the practitioner. Mental health practitioners needs to scrutinise and evaluate the effectiveness of their own practice in supporting improved outcomes in a more proportionate number of people from BME backgrounds. The Racism Diagnostic and Review Tool can be used to assess dispassionately the contributions made by individual practitioners based on what they are able to demonstrate.

CHAPTER 4

RECOVERY-FOCUSED CARE PLANNING

One source of confusion that arises when planning to meet the needs of people from BME groups is the tendency to think that this just means offering a culturally specific service. There may be occasions when a culturally specific service or intervention would be helpful but the focus should be on aiding recovery, as it should be for all service users. BME service users state that offering a culturally specific service must be a means to this end and not the end itself (Bowl 2007b). Offering a culturally specific service is different to offering an ethnically matched worker. The latter approach may not deliver the changes expected if the processes and interventions being used are undifferentiated.

Definition

The process of recovery focused care planning (RFCP) follows on from the assessments process which is described, in Chapter 3. The pursuit of recovery first requires a clear understanding of what this means. Governmental bodies have published various documents to help clarify what is meant by mental health recovery. The emphasis is not purely on being symptom-free but on recovering a position in society where the inner strengths of individuals are capitalised upon so that they are enabled to meet their full potential, within the context of their mental health experiences (Department of Health 2004a, 2005c; Social Care Institute for Excellence 2007a). Recovery is an ongoing process. It is not an absolute position that is arrived at. A professional athlete may recover from a torn ligament sufficiently well to sprint and win medals but may eschew their long-jump career because his body can no longer sustain the impact of a heavy landing. An individual recovering from a mental health problem may be like one athlete who is forever out of international competition or another who regains some but not all abilities. Some recover with increased determination and strength.

Conflicts with the recovery-focused approach

Society, policy-makers and government place requirements upon mental health services that at best run parallel to the recovery approach and at worst directly contradict it. Practitioners on the front line are told to make risk assessments and for these to be paramount. The press vilifies staff and services when things go wrong, even where detailed and sophisticated inquiries demonstrate that service failings were not a causal factor (*Evening Standard* 2005). Services are therefore risk averse and are more inclined to focus on containment, public protection and risk management (*Community Care Magazine* 2006). Recovery-focused care planning in this context is fraught. It is possible to promote positive risk-taking but individual practitioners are often only willing to do so where the organisation is clear in its policy and behaviours that this approach is welcomed and that workers will not be left exposed if something does go wrong (Department of Health 2007a; Langan and Lindow 2004). The recovery-focused approach does not require practitioners to turn a blind eye to risk or to understate it. The approach requires honesty in discussions with service users. Planning for the journey of recovery needs to take into account the impact of the service user's behaviour in relation to risk. For example, an honest discussion can be had about the cost to the service user if he or she perpetrates an injury to another person. Problems caused by a failure to consider risk were highlighted well in the report into the care and treatment of Christopher Clunis (Ritchie, Dick and Lingham 1994).

Implementing recovery-focused care planning

Ethnicity, race and culture complicate the ability of practitioners to work within the recovery framework. The challenges that arise from the conflicting demands placed on mental health services are accentuated by the salience given to negative aspects of the lives of individuals from BME groups, as highlighted in Chapter 3. Within this context RFCP must include the following aspects:

- an assessment that is comprehensive, underpinned by a critical approach

- clarity about the ends being pursued at that particular point in time

- clarity about the obstacles

- exploration of all potential means of achieving recovery

- investment in the relationship as a vehicle for change.

The features of an assessment that is comprehensive and underpinned by a critical approach were discussed in Chapter 3. The other points will be discussed in turn.

Clarity about the ends being pursued

The concept of holistic assessments and planning needs to reflect the various aspects of people's lives:

- physical

- spiritual

- identity

- social

- economic

- mental.

(Beresford *et al.* 2005)

Mental health services refer to various terms such as self-directed care, person-centred planning, user-led planning. Personalisation is the dominant theme in government health and social care policy (Department of Health 2006, 2008b). This refers to arrangements that enable service users to design bespoke care packages to meet their needs, for example through the transfer of some of the commissioning budgets to individuals. An expectation is placed upon practitioners that they will take into account the range of aspects of people's lives when they implement the Care Programme Approach in mental health (Harrison 2007). The Care Programme Approach is the national mechanism for ensuring elements of care and treatment are coordinated and based on robust assessments. Care planning should support service users to move to greater control, for example though having personalised budgets. The reality, however, is that the extent to which staff work with service users to achieve goals in all aspects of their lives varies (Sainsbury Centre for Mental Health 2007). This is due to a number of factors:

- a lack of opportunities/services for meeting a wider range of service user needs

- low expectations of service users

- loss of hopefulness because of constant exposure to people stuck in the system, not those whose lives most demonstrate triumph and recovery

- lack of capacity (for various reasons such as large amounts of paperwork, many cases, inefficient use of time)

- a narrow focus on risk management

- stereotypical views about what people may be able to achieve

- poor levels of skills to explore a range of aspects of people's lives (e.g. the impact of racism)

- poor supervision and personal development.

(Bennett, Kalathil and Keating 2007; Bhui 2002; DeSisto *et al.* 1995; Fernando 1995; Office of the Deputy Prime Minister 2004; Sainsbury Centre for Mental Health 2002a)

The impact of these areas of weakness on BME groups is likely to be greater than the impact for white groups. Low expectations and stereotypical views are multiplied by ERC. The absence of choice in local services (for example the BME voluntary sector) compounds the problem.

BOX 4.1 ILLUSTRATION

Anne, a manager of a community mental health team (CMHT), led a discussion with her team after she had attended a conference on race and mental health. She asked her team members to reflect on their caseloads. She made no reference to race or ethnicity though she knew that together they would look at the outcome in relation to these. On average (the mean) workers had 27 cases and on average six were from a BME background. The exercise that Anne gave her team was as follows.

Team members were asked to consider all service users on their case loads and to score a number of factors on a 4-point scale, where I was a weak association and 4 was the strongest association. The factors were:

- I find them easy to communicate with
- I find them affable
- They are cooperative
- I feel comfortable in their presence
- They appreciate me
- We have on occasions had a laugh.

After this Anne asked the team to note the ethnicity of the service user to whom each of the scores related.

Of the seven care coordinators who took part, all (apart from Eric) had a pattern where for the BME service users there was an overwhelmingly weaker positive association with the statements above. For most staff, about half of their BME service users were scored 2 or under for all six statements. Of their 21 (on average) white service users on caseloads only three or four had equally 'poor' scores. (Eric scored very weakly for virtually his entire caseload.)

Each team member's scores for the six statements were converted into an unweighted average (totalled and divided by 6). The team aggregate scores were as follows:

BME service users scoring 2 or less: 24 out of 45 (53.3%)

White service users scoring 2 or less: 31 out of 144 (21.5%)

The team discussed the reasons for scoring in the way they did. The low scores for BME service users scores were because the care coordinators felt:

- language was a real barrier for some
- some came across as being surly
- some showed an unwillingness to comply with any agreement
- some were angry all the time
- there were others for whom there was no sense of a relationship.

Anne concluded that the team had an unwitting bias against the BME service users. Though all of their reasons for scoring as they did were recognisable, she felt that the outcome was poorer levels of engagement and that the 'therapeutic alliance' was weaker. This, they concluded, would potentially lead to less energetic advocacy on behalf of the service users from BME backgrounds. They were convinced that it would definitely lead to poorer recovery focused care planning.

This was corroborated in the team performance information, which showed that for BME service users repeat admissions were more frequent and the proportion of service users in work, education and volunteering was poorer than for white service users.

The team concluded that though they would not, as individuals, consider themselves as racist they were not convinced that as a team they were not institutionally racist. They started a programme of change that they hoped would combat these patterns, whatever the rationale behind them.

Clarity about the obstacles to RFCP

The illustration in Box 4.1 shows some of the obstacles to RFCP with people from BME backgrounds. A practitioner who, with the service user, is clear about the goals being pursued, will need to understand what may stand in the way of these being achieved. Despite the conceptualisation by Anne's team that the problems resulted from the presentations by service users there were three aspects at work:

- what the worker brought to the relationship

- what the service user brought to the dynamic

- conflicts in policy

- the absence of, or failure to utilise, alternative services or supports.

The need to understand how the negative trends in research are reflected in the content of referrals was highlighted in Chapter 3. Safeguards may be introduced through knowing and understanding the default position, i.e. what will happen if specific measures are not taken to try to counter the trends. This type of approach is also needed in care planning. RFCP needs to take account of areas of raised risk of disparities for people from BME backgrounds.

WHAT THE WORKER BRINGS

Training equips a worker to know the correct things to say and how to behave in a way that is consistent with the principles and value of the profession (Bennett *et al.* 2007). Training courses, however, are usually unable to address deep down likes and dislikes. Most workers are trained with a working assumption that if they are provided with information and given some advice on skills, good practice will follow. The main exception is in psychotherapy, where it is acknowledged that the internal world of the therapist needs to be explored and worked through thoroughly before they can effectively work with the client (Thomas 1992). It is striking, however, that even in this field ERC were not dealt with effectively for years and even now, the concept of culture-free therapy abounds (Moodley and Palmer 2006).

Practitioners will have feelings that are at odds with the best standards of their profession. These cannot be dictated by the wishes of individual workers, their trainers, their organisations or the courts. Just telling people what to think or how to behave will not make them stop feeling certain things. This is an important acknowledgement in the context of ERC. When can a worker say that she finds African people too loud or that she hates visiting Asian families because she cannot understand the accents? When is it safe for workers to talk about things that are stereotypes and taboo? When are they able to express that based on their experience they believe certain stereotypes are accurate and that despite training there are some norms of other ethical groups they dislike? Some workers benefit from safe relationships with a therapist or a good mentor or friend but often even in these contexts this kind of material is avoided. The consequence is that thoughts, feelings and beliefs that remain unexplored emerge in subversive ways (Cooper *et al.* 2006). It is no surprise, therefore, that subtle forms of discriminatory behaviour seep out into practice and compound problems of service user experience and outcomes.

The exercise in Box 4.2 attempts to prompt a practitioner into open and honest internal discussion. It requires workers to look at subjects that they would rather assume are not part of their internal world. Bhui (2002, p.223) makes the point that 'not all practitioners will be able to meet the demands of such self-reflection and self-appraisal'.

WHAT THE SERVICE USER BRINGS

Recovery-focused care planning is a partnership between the worker and the service user. The service user's feelings and behaviours have an impact on this. McLean *et al.* (2003, p.664), in their study of African Caribbean service users' experiences, state, 'racism was clearly perceived to structure the treatment of African Caribbean community members, and this perception strongly discouraged people from approaching mental health services due to an anticipation of racist stereotyping and treatment'.

BOX 4.2 EXERCISE

Reflect, then make a note of your private and honest responses to these prompts. Think about who you are, your likes and dislikes and your feelings about the demands made on you at work. Imagine what you would say or what your behaviour would look like if you were unrestrained in relation to the impulses you feel in relation to:

- difficulty you have in understanding accents
- the volume or volubility of speech
- families becoming involved in cases
- mannerisms that you find culturally alien
- what is perceived as inappropriate sexualised behaviour
- frustration you feel as a result of having your attempts to help rejected
- smells that you find unattractive, e.g. those associated with African, Caribbean or Asian foods or with skin or beauty products
- a style of dress that you find alien or odd.

Think about your work with service users from other ethnic backgrounds and consider whether there is any leakage of these impulses in to your work.

This difficult exercise may lead you to unearth some feelings for which you may require some help in addressing. On the contrary, you may get to the brink of considering some items and then to recoil because it is uncomfortable. It is important that you note your reactions as these will also help you to be clearer about how you have been dealing with these issues in the past.

If you feel disturbed and require help to work through your feelings it is important that you speak with your supervisor about the need for a safe context in which to do this. It could be through a number or routes, for example an external mentor, the occupational counselling service or professional supervision.

Despite the attempts of academics to highlight the non-racist credentials of services (Singh and Burns 2006), practitioners will still need to be equipped to work with people who are angry, disillusioned or disengaged because of their perceptions of services. The starting point must be where both the worker and the service user are and not where they wish one or the other to be.

It is striking that in the Joint Position Paper *A Common Purpose: Recovery in Future Mental Health Services* (Social Care Institute for Excellence 2007a) the only quotes from the BME focus group relate to their concerns about the recovery-focused approach in mental health services. Members of the focus group that helped to inform the development of the paper felt concerned that the recovery approach would threaten their existing coping strategies.

There is no single commentary or perspective that represents the view of all BME communities. A recurrent theme in literature is the extent to which services are viewed with suspicion or are detested. The qualitative study as part of the government's Count Me In census of inpatients highlights the extent to which BME groups report negative experiences and feel negatively about mental health services (Mental Health Act Commission 2006).

A serious obstacle to RFCP is the extent to which BME service users have poor expectations of services.

POLICY CONFLICTS

A conflict exists in the polarities in policy: standardisation and individualisation. Standardisation is pursued in an attempt to create greater productivity and efficiencies in modelling and delivering services (Audit Commission 2006; Fairbairn 2007; Sainsbury Centre for Mental Health 2004). Individualisation is pursued through the 'personalisation agenda' in the White Paper *Our Health Our Care Our Say* and the Green Paper *Transforming Social Care* (Department of Health 2006, 2008b).

These conflicts extend to the need to take into account the differences in relation to ERC. Research evidence is consistent in showing that there are differences in pathways to services according to ethnic background. The experiences of BME groups (black groups in particular) mean that they often arrive at services with a more complex set of needs (Bhugra, Harding and Lippett 2004; Morgan *et al.* 2005a, 2005b). Given this situation, which is used as an argument for why outcomes are different, it is peculiar that the service response to black people is no different to that for white people. It is the equivalent of operating an accident and emergency department that attempts to ensure fairness by operating a ticketing system so that people are seen in strict order. Showing a disregard for the difference in presentation between someone with multiple stab wounds and someone with a broken wrist would be bizarre. Supported by findings, for example by Morgan *et al.* (2005b), mental health services recognise the differences in the complexity of need at presentation between ethnic groups but take pride in providing standardised (colour-blind) approaches.

In English schools the concept of 'added value' is measured, to acknowledge that not everyone starts from the same baseline but that institutions should be able to measure the difference that they make. In addition to overall academic outcomes for each pupil, the 'value added score' provides useful information. It gives a measure for the progress made academically. Mental health services struggle to find a way to measure progress or added value (Fairbairn 2007). Singh *et al.* (2007) conducted a meta-analysis on 19 studies into compulsory admissions for people from BME backgrounds and noted that 'the increasing detention rate across time, with lower rates for first-episode illness, suggests that the relationship between black and minority ethnic patients and mental health services deteriorates over time' (p.103). On the basis of this 19-study review it appears that services add less value to BME services users compared with white service users.

Services need to reflect on whether there is an unspoken complicit acceptance that BME service users are unlikely to gain much from services. If this undercurrent runs through services it will affect the expectations of professionals and will contaminate the extent to which they work with service users on RFCP.

THE ABSENCE OF ALTERNATIVES

Another obstacle to RFCP is limited access to alternative services and models for considering the service users' problems. Chapter 9 explores different way in which people view their experiences of mental health problems and refers to critiques of traditional psychiatry by Blackman (2007), Read, Hammersley and Rudegeair (2007), Romme and Escher (1993) and Thomas and Bracken (2005). The UK mental health system is constructed on the basis of psychiatry and alternatives are not given legitimacy. Third-sector BME organisations may be in a position to offer alternative models of mental health problems and service designs but these are not well resourced or supported to flourish (Fernando 2005). Few professionals openly operate with alternative models within statutory mental health services.

Exploration of all potential means of achieving recovery

Mental health services operate in a climate of increased pursuit of efficiency (Audit Commission 2006). In this context practitioners are required to be more resourceful in finding ways of helping to meet the needs of service users. A worker needs to be active in researching options, advocating, brokering, negotiating and arranging alternatives. RFCP recognises that interventions of mental health services are potentially just a small component of what might contribute to recovery. For some it is worse than this; statutory mental health services are felt to be an obstacle (Office of the Deputy Prime Minister 2004).

Effective practitioners must therefore avail themselves of all potential sources of support:

- personalised budgets for service users to achieve self-directed care

- BME-specific third sector

- general third-sector mental health services

- statutory sector BME-specific services

- statutory sector generic services

- community-based universal services

- self-help approaches

- families and 'carers'

- faith groups.

Many studies have identified that BME service users often seek alternatives to mainstream mental health services (Bhui and Sashidharan 2003; Bowl 2007a, 2007b; Chantler 2002; Department of Heath 2005b; Sainsbury Centre for Mental Health 2002a). The development of alternatives does not, however, excuse statutory mental health services from the need to provide appropriate and responsive services (Department of Health 2005b).

BME-SPECIFIC THIRD SECTOR

Referrals to BME-specific services are often considered as a way of meeting the cultural needs of service users. It is seldom clear what is meant by this. Based on the definition of culture (see Chapter 1) the assumptions being made by referrers are often flawed. An Asian centre may be predominantly Punjabi or Gujarati or may be more expert at working across a range of faiths or languages. The scope of religious or linguistic competence is often not explored at the point of referral. These concerns could be applied to the ethnic differences in any racial group, for example a 'black day service' may be attempting to meet the needs of African and African Caribbean people from many countries or islands that have different cultures and languages.

Further to benefits arising from linguistic and cultural similarity, BME-specific services potentially offer:

- a sense of shared identity and belonging

- a shared recognition of difference in relation to the white majority or other ethnic groups

- a preparedness to celebrate cultures and the knowledge to do so

- more open discussion about the impact of race on experience and outcomes

- at their best, specific forms of therapy or support that keep race central.

The case study in Box 4.3 shows an attempt by a worker to address ERC by making a referral to a BME-specific service. Three different interpretations of this are presented.

BOX 4.3 ILLUSTRATION

Abdul Rahman is 23 years old. He had been working in an outlet of a major chain of computer retailers. He had worked in their service department for 18 months and was well regarded. His access to regular money whilst still living at home had enabled him to pursue a social life with his friends, clubbing and drinking. Abdul had attempted to secure his own small flat but each time he visited advertised accommodation he was told that either he needed a bigger deposit than was stated in the newspaper advert or that someone had looked before him and the prospective landlord was awaiting confirmation that he would be accepting.

Over the period of a few months Abdul became increasingly tense and this culminated in a fight at a nightclub. Though this did not stop his fun-loving lifestyle his friends reported that his drink consumption had increased and his behaviour was uncharacteristically aggressive. His brother, Mo, told his friends that he was not surprised that Abdul had an aggressive streak, as their father was very strict when they were children and he tried to force them to remain devout Muslims. Mo said that Abdul often seethed with anger whilst being silently compliant. Both siblings stopped attending mosque in their early teens.

A series of events in which Abdul was disorientated and highly aroused led to him having a three-week admission to psychiatric hospital. Though no final diagnosis had been given the prevailing views amongst professionals was that this would be bipolar affective disorder. Having made attempts to return to work, Abdul found that his concentration was not good enough to focus on the intricate tasks he was required to do. He resigned and spent his days at home.

Harry, his care coordinator in the community mental health team (CMHT) for the last ten weeks, was keen to ensure that Abdul did not compound his mental health problems by remaining isolated. He also felt that being at home for hours with his parents was causing Abdul distress. As part of their care planning, Harry suggested that Abdul might like to attend the Asian men's group at the day centre as a means of developing social contact. They also discussed trying to get a flat. These two elements, along with supporting Abdul to discuss his medication with the psychiatrist, represented the care plan.

As part of the CMHT development, the manager commissioned a group of specialists in BME mental health and asked them to help team members explore their practice. These specialists were able to speak with service users who gave their consent to receive suggestions for potential service improvements. Ade, a BME mental health specialist, reviewed some of Harry's practice. He also spoke with Abdul. The outcome of their discussions follows.

Harry's perspective: Harry was keen to prevent Abdul from becoming a 'career mental health patient'; by this he meant that he didn't want him to become stuck in the system. The priority in Harry's mind was to help Abdul partake in activities that were outside of the mental health system. He also wanted to be mindful of Abdul's ethnicity and to show that he was attuned to this.

Abdul's perspective: Abdul's head was swimming. As far as he was concerned he was just having a bad time when weird things were going on in his life. He could not quite understand why he was being seen by mental health services. The idea of a referral to the Asian men's group mystified him. He considered this as the kind of activity his uncles would engage in.

Ade's perspective: Ade's feedback to Harry was that the referral to the Asian men's group did not show an appreciation of Abdul's unique needs, taking into account his age, etc. Ade also pointed out that there were indicators of racism or at least that Abdul believed he was experiencing racism (i.e. in relation to his attempts to find a flat). This issue was not explored, giving an

> impression that Abdul's experiences of racism were not valid and were unimportant in the context of the therapeutic relationship. Ade suggested that as a consequence Abdul might feel as though Harry would never engage with him fully if it meant dealing with uncomfortable issues, and would potentially reciprocate this. Ade said that Harry's referral to the Asian men's group could be seen as stereotypical. An act that was intended to be positive was undermined because of what was communicated by the avoidance of racism. Ade assessed that Harry was content to deal with race but not with racism.

Staff working in mental health services sometimes have aspirations about what they would like to offer in their work with service users, which they find difficulty in realising. For example Evans *et al.* (2006) identified high stress levels and dissatisfaction amongst social workers in mental health services. This was partly as a result of the limits placed upon them in relation to meeting the needs of service users in a way that is consistent with their professional values. It is evident from the Singh *et al.* (2007) meta-analysis that there are variations in impact on readmissions according to ethnicity. Professionals could benefit from reflecting on how their own interactions contribute to the variability of impacts.

Investment in the relationship as a vehicle for change
The strength of the service user/practitioner relationship is a critical aspect of RFCP. Chapter 5 is dedicated to exploring this in detail.

Conclusion
Recovery-focused care planning is a partnership between the service user and the practitioner. The relationship is the hub of this process and both parties bring elements that need to be consciously considered. RFCP highlights some conflicts in policy and how services are designed. Practitioners are required to manage competing demands whilst avoiding the charges levied by service users that workers are obstacles rather than assets in the recovery process for service users.

BOX 4.4 EXERCISE

Identify one service user from a BME background on your caseload for whom, upon reflection, you think the care plan is narrower than it should be. Consider the steps that you have taken to work with them on recovery-focused goals.

List the outcomes that you consider would be desirable for this person. Think about as many aspects of the person's life as possible, for example:

- mental health
- physical health
- spirituality (not just organised religion)
- accommodation
- friendships
- family relationships
- intimate sexual relationships
- work
- leisure
- self-care
- physical appearance
- sense of identity – race/ethnicity
- sense of identity – gender
- sense of identity – sexuality
- pursuit of justice for things that happened in the person's past.

Complete a table like Table 4.1 below.

Table 4.1 Template: Working towards recovery with service users

Outcomes	Service user's view about issues	My view about issues	What's in the care plan	What I could help with

This exercise will take time. It may be something to which you return.

When completing the exercise think about the following:

- Have you discussed all of these outcomes and do you return to them periodically?
- How do you deal with the differences of view between you and the service user?

In the fifth column consider:

- things you can do directly
- ways in which you could adapt your behaviour
- ways in which you might challenge others
- ways in which you might encourage the service user.

Specific questions that might arise for you:

- As a mental health professional what is your role in these areas?
- How do you balance recovery-focused care planning with the duty of care/obligations of public protection?
- How do you give the service user the lead but still prompt progress in areas (including topics where they actively exclude you)?
- To what extent do your personal beliefs cause conflict and how is this handled?
- What do you do about a lack of resources to address certain areas (time, your knowledge and skills, or services)?
- How do you challenge your own organisation and other agencies about poor or discriminatory policies and practice?

CHAPTER 5

QUALITY RELATIONSHIPS IN THE DELIVERY OF CARE PLANS

Around three-quarters of mental health trusts' budgets are spent on staff, the highest proportion being on front-line staff (Audit Commission 2006). Mental health services rely heavily on front-line staff and the quality of relationships is critical in pursuit of their aims of improving outcomes for service users.

Chapter 2 set out variances in experiences and outcomes for groups of service. Factors affecting the relationship relate to:

- experiences prior to entering mental health services

- differences in the people (personalities)

- differences in mental health presentations

- differences in response to physical interventions

- differences in response to non-physical inputs such as the therapeutic relationship therapy

- variations in how physical interventions are applied

- variations in how psychosocial inputs are provided.

In relation to BME groups specifically, various studies have covered four broad areas:

- pathways (Bhugra 2003, 2004; Morgan *et al.* 2005a, 2005b).

- presentations (Cooper *et al.* 2008; Sainsbury Centre for Mental Health 2002a.)

- experience of physical interventions (Mental Health Act Commission 2008)

- access to psychosocial support (Raleigh *et al.* 2007).

Organisations cannot undo the past for those currently in services but they must work with others to attempt to change pathways for those not yet within them. For people currently in services mental health workers attempt to support recovery by focusing on change in four mains areas: the patient/service user; themselves as the professionals; physical interventions; and psychosocial supports (the 4 Ps). These are set out in Figure 5.1.

Patient/service user	Professional
Entrenched patterns	Personal prejudices
Presentations	Attributes
	Knowledge and skills
Physical	**Psychosocial**
Medication	Psychological therapies
Restraints	Employment
Electroconvulsive therapy	Leisure

Figure 5.1 The 4 Ps in the therapeutic relationship

Rationale for focusing on the relationship

The relationship between the service user and the professional is central to all of the potential inputs and outcomes in the work of practitioners. The study in America by Cooper *et al.* (2006) profoundly deconstructs components of the worker/service user relationship and points to the relationship as being the fulcrum for change.

Toxic Interactions Theory (Box 2.1) draws on conclusions from various studies into disparities and emphasises that the potential for change resides in the relationship between service users from BME backgrounds and practitioners. Shapiro and Shapiro (1982), in their meta-analysis of research, conclude that the quality of the therapeutic relationship was the consistent variable in outcome effectiveness of different psychological interventions.

Relationship centrality

In the work of mental health practitioners the relationship has an impact on each of the focuses for change, the 4 Ps noted in Figure 5.1. Figure 5.2 depicts the relationship as the container for change.

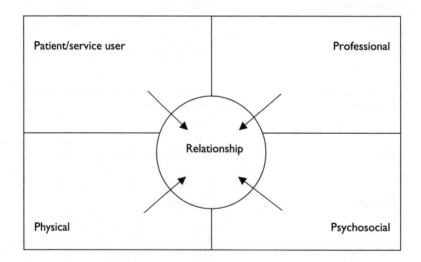

Figure 5.2 Relationship as the container for change in the 4 Ps

The role of specific interventions is often the focus of attention in seeking solutions to the challenges arising from the disparities for people from BME backgrounds. Miranda *et al.* (2005) review psychological interventions and describe how modifications can increase their effectiveness for people from BME backgrounds. They identify the need to amend approaches to take into account the cultural norms of the group, though they do ponder the mechanism for ensuring fidelity to the intervention whilst doing so. For example, conceptualisations of individuality may differ between cultural groups, or the concept of family may be stronger in some cultural groups and this may have introduced bias in the design approach. Service models are also given attention and these too are the subject of research.

Solutions are not always found in interventions and service models. Pharmacological interventions are given primacy in the statutory service response to mental health problems because of the perceived strength of evidence of their efficacy and assumed effectiveness. This robustness is assumed because the body of evidence has been developed through randomised controlled trials (RCT), which Slade and Priebe (2001) highlight as being the gold standard of research methodologies. Slade and Priebe (2001), however, attempted to dispel the myth that generalised predictions can be made about reliability in the use of medicines. Kikkert *et al.* (2006) looked at the social component in the use of medication. They tackled the issue of adherence and highlighted the fact that 50 per cent of people on psychiatric medications do not adhere to regime. They demonstrated that the way in which medication is viewed and used has an impact on its effectiveness. One of the suggestions to improve adherence was a focus on the *therapeutic relationship*. Another study that demonstrated that having an RCT evidence base is not its own a predictor or of outcomes is the REACT study (Killapsy *et al.* 2006). This indicated that despite an evidence base of success eleswhere the assertive outreach model did not demonstrate reduced readmission rates and use of inpatient beds in the UK, as had been the hope of policy-makers. It did, however, identify greater service user satisfaction with services and engagement.

A major obstacle to improving outcomes for BME groups is that there is not a body of evidence from RCTs about what works. It is clear, however, from the Slade and Priebe (2001), Kikkert *et al.* (2006) and Killaspy *et al.* (2006) studies that RCT research evidence does not hold the sole key to discovering what might achieve desired outcomes.

The repeated hypotheses of researchers, that the quality of relationships may hold the key to improvements in outcomes for people from BME backgrounds (e.g. McLean *et al.* 2003; Sainsbury Centre for Mental Health 2002a; Singh *et al.* 2007), provides some hope for practitioners.

Counter arguments

The national survey analysed by Raleigh *et al.* (2007) includes a set of questions within the 'relationship domain'. Raleigh *et al.* (2007) identify that the responses of service users from BME backgrounds are on a par with those from white people. This raises the question as to why BME groups routinely report poor satisfaction with services (Bowl 2007a, 2007b; Mental Health Act Commission 2006; Parkman *et al.* 1997; Sainsbury Centre for Mental Health 2002a; Wilson 1993) but respond to questions in a national survey about concrete experiences in a way that does not indicate such differences. It is probable that the metrics used by the survey to assess quality of experience failed to capture the true experience of BME groups. Raleigh *et al.* (2007) highlight that responses to the national service user survey demonstrate proportionately less access to therapeutic services by people from BME backgrounds but at the same time highlight no statistically significant difference in satisfaction rates. A weakness in the Raleigh *et al.* (2007) study is the lack of analysis of the qualitative narratives submitted by service users in the Healthcare Commission's survey. The survey by the Healthcare Commission (with the Mental Health Act Commission) of inpatients included a report on follow-up interviews with patients in 2005 (Mental Health Act Commission 2006), which highlighted major concerns raised by BME service users, proving a rich source of narratives about actual (negative) experiences. These included the lack of respect they felt they had received or time they were given. Both of these were reported more frequently than for white inpatients.

Trust

Therapeutic relationships that ignore the veracious nature of racism undermine trust. Cooper *et al.* (2006) highlight trust as a key component in the relationship needed in work with people from BME backgrounds. Workers are often more content dealing with culture (see Box 4.3). Cultural awareness is important but can easily be managed through learning and development. Considering race and racism with BME service users (whatever the background of the worker) takes more than the recollection of cultural norms. Silence on the subject, or worse, sloppy handling of racism, is a form of communication and it is sometimes greeted with silence in return. Cooper *et al.* (2008) identify that service users from BME backgrounds did not disproportionately locate the cause of the mental health problems in racism but rather, in disadvantage. The fact that more people from BME backgrounds experience disadvantage has, however, been unequivocally likened to various forms of racism (Commission for Racial Equality 2007).

BOX 5.1 EXERCISE

Think about how the relationship between you and a current service user from a BME background has changed over the past 18 months. Write down:

- the differences you see in the service user
- differences in your feelings towards him or her
- differences in your behaviour towards him or her
- changes in access to, and experience of the service user's physical and psychosocial support.

Consider the relationship as a catalyst for change. Compare and contrast the relationship at key points in time:

- now
- six months ago
- twelve months ago
- eighteen months ago.

For these points in time note down:

- the conversations you had about goals
- how racism had been discussed
- discussions that had taken place about the service user's identity (in the broadest sense – e.g. gender, age, sexuality, experience of abuse)
- how much more was known about them as a person – e.g. the service user's thoughts and his or her feelings.
- How they responded to you exploring these issues?

How has your increased knowledge and understanding affected your interpretation of the service user's mental health problems and the reasons for him or her using services?

Obstacles to effective relationships

It is often assumed in mental health services that core skills such as listening and interviewing are well established amongst the workforce. The new system of pay and rewards for staff introduced into the UK National Health Service in 2004 (Agenda for Change) uses the Knowledge and Skills Framework (KSF) as a criteria-based approach to setting learning and development targets (Department of Health 2004b). Despite the well-defined approach, the KSF is unable to unearth some basic skills gaps. The KSF was introduced into an existing workforce, which meant that it would have been difficult for existing workers to identify (with their managers) that they were not achieving very basic standards. It is difficult to revisit learning and development needs once there has been a reinforcement of an assumed level of competence. It is often not until errors occur that the scale of skills and knowledge gaps becomes apparent. Perhaps with regard to ERC it is the persistence of disparities that highlights the problem.

Talking about racial and cultural discrimination is often charged with fear, anger, shame, denial and avoidance (Singer 2006). Practitioners are often reluctant to deal with these. The field of psychological therapies is more versed in considering the dynamics of relationships and provides useful paradigms for exploring the fear and feelings that are aroused. Psychotherapists were also late in incorporating considerations of race and culture in their work, a theme discussed variously in the book edited by Moodley and Palmer (2006).

One of the strengths of the training for psychological therapies, and psychodynamic psychotherapy in particular, is the attention given to the therapist understanding his or her own motivations and drives; his or her own fears and vulnerabilities. Cooper *et al.* (2006) conceptualise this as the 'clinician–self' relationship.

Obstacles to better relationship-building with people from BME backgrounds relate to:

- poor recognition of the practitioner's influences on the relationship

- assumed knowledge

- over-enthusiasm

- failure to give due regard to ERC

- behaviour that is incongruent with the rhetoric

- being overwhelmed by the challenges in relation to ERC.

Poor recognition of the practitioner's influences on the relationship

Services and practitioners often present problems in achieving outcomes in care planning as failures of service users; either they have failed to engage or comply.

The relationship between the worker and the service user has an influence on outcomes. Cooper *et al.* 2006, Griffith 1977 and Liggan and Kay (2006) explore the issues as experienced separately by white and black practitioners and make the point that the considerations of personal influence are not restricted only to white people.

Not only will workers need to consider their own values, prejudices and fears, they will also need to be mindful of the possible ways in which they may be viewed by the service user (Thomas 1992). Bringing the unspoken into open discussion, if handled effectively, can liberate the relationship to be a medium for change. This is not always straightforward. It takes skill and confidence for white workers to ask about the impact of their race on the relationship. They may worry that the black service user will have expectations unrealistically raised that they are able have a black worker if they wish. A black worker may erroneously conclude that the shared identity of being from a BME background creates a natural alliance, mitigating the need to discuss race. A consequence of the absence of discussions about race and racism is that they have an impact on the relationship but remain unacknowledged.

Despite recruitment and selection procedures workers may be appointed who harbour views that they know would be perceived in many circles as being racist. They may be aware that they dislike a particular ethnic group but try to keep this separate from any relationship required as part of the job.

The absence of routine exploration of workers' thoughts and feelings about race in a safe place creates an obstacle. It would be foolhardy for workers to invite discussion with a service user about something that is personal and emotionally difficult for them to contain (Leary 2006). It is nonetheless limiting to work with a service user from a BME background without the confidence and abilities to speak about race and ethnicity.

The relationships between individuals typify the relations in the wider social world. The power held by white people at a societal level is reflected in individual relationships (Banton 1967; Liggan and Kay 2006). It should not be a surprise, therefore, that tensions about race surface in the working relationship. Leary (2006) notes that the practitioner/service user relationships in the entire health and social care context are fertile for eruptions around race and racism.

Assumed knowledge

When forming relationships, problems can arise if assumptions are made about the individual, based on real or perceived ethnic identity. At its crudest this would be described as stereotyping. Each individual will have his or her own way of expressing his or her ethnic identity. The way in which race features in people's lives will vary from one individual to another. Thomas (1992) discusses pre-transference and its impact on relationships. He refers to the experience of young people who feel that their therapists act as though they can predict who they are, supposedly based on having previously met people similar to them.

Assumptions about an individual or group may be informed by many different sources. Workers may have friends or acquaintances from a particular ethnic background. They may have lived in a country related to the service user's heritage or may have received cultural awareness training. BME practitioners may be from the same or similar ethnic background and feel that they are familiar with the perspectives of the service user. Whatever the source of the perceived knowledge, this may lead to assumptions that detract from the professional curiosity that is essential to underpin any relationship-building (see Box 6.4).

Individuals may either be immersed in something that denotes their culture or they may position themselves outside of this (Sue and Sue 1990). A person's idea of ethnic identity may be different to that of someone from within the same family. Someone may not overtly celebrate his or her ethnic, cultural or racial identity but may be fiercely critical of anything that he or she perceives as being racist. In short, there are no alternatives to asking and investigating these matters if workers are to build good relationships with service users.

Over-enthusiasm

People are often suspicious about the motivations of someone outside their group who champions their cause. Men who label themselves as ardent feminists are often treated with some scepticism. White people who fiercely champion racial equality are viewed as trying to compensate for problems of their own, such as guilt or an awareness of their own propensity to be racist (Jewson and Mason 1992).

There is no way of defining 'over-enthusiasm'. The term implies that there is an optimal level of enthusiasm or an acceptable range. In reality, the concept is well reflected in discourse but no system has been developed to determine over-enthusiasm or under enthusiasm. In the absence of an absolute measure, the guiding principle must be the relationship itself. Being over-enthusiastic implies that a worker is insistent irrespective of the wishes of the service user. The desire to have more open conversations about race and racism is a consistent theme in studies of BME perspectives in mental health (Parkman *et al.* 1997; Sainsbury Centre for Mental Health 2002a; Wilson 1993). Workers should be confident in the legitimacy of their attempt to discuss a subject but must retain their service user-led approach (Mearns and Thorne 1988).

Failure to give due regard to ethnicity, race and culture

Ignoring race within the relationship undermines the ability of the worker to tackle issues of racism in the life of the service user. There are two problems with this. First, the evasion of issues to do with race and racism can undermine trust and therefore weaken engagement. Second, research is increasingly pointing to the impact of racism and discrimination as a significant factor in the higher rates of diagnosed mental health problems in BME groups (Cooper *et al.* 2008; Veling *et al.* 2007). In 1987 the *Guardian* newspaper ran an article entitled 'Is racism driving blacks out of their minds' (*Guardian* 1987) and 15 years later the *British Journal of Psychiatry* published 'Does racial discrimination cause mental illness?' (Chakraborty and McKenzie 2002). Twenty years after the *Guardian* article, a Dutch research article, which referred to the UK situation, hypothesised about the same issue (Veling *et al.* 2007).

Behaviour that is incongruent with the rhetoric

Service users will experience mistrust if workers tell them that they are aware of race and racism but do not demonstrate this awareness in their behaviours. Statements of a commitment to tackling discrimination or a shared outrage at injustices that are not consistently converted into action will lead to charges that the worker is disingenuous or duplicitous. BME service users report their observations about this in the study by Bowl (2007b). It would be a perverse outcome for workers to diminish the boldness of their statements about race equality to avoid this charge. A more ethical approach would be for workers to assess the extent to which they achieve or fall short of their own aspirations for tackling race equality.

Dealing with feedback is challenging. The requirements of regulatory bodies are increasingly leaning towards more regular mechanisms for gleaning service user feedback. This is seen in the Healthcare Commission's assessment against the *Standards for Better Health* (Department of Health 2004c) and the Audit Commission's *Auditors' Local Evaluation* (Audit Commission 2007). Both regimes set standards for the management and governance of a range of areas of an NHS Trust's business (the latter focusing on the use of resources). Organisations are assessed and rated against specific criteria and are prompted by certain standards to become more focused on responding to service user and stakeholder feedback. Success can only be achieved by cascading the approach through the organisation, to staff on the front line. Workers need to be prepared to seek feedback and to handle the responses appropriately so that there can be a greater consistency between what is said and what is done in relation to ERC.

Being overwhelmed by the challenges in relation to ethnicity, race and culture

Many workers in mental health services are aware of the gross variations in BME service user experience and outcomes. Along with this knowledge is awareness that for over 30 years researchers, academics and service providers have struggled to identify solutions. It is not surprising, given the scale of the problems and the lack of precision about solutions, that front-line workers feel overwhelmed at times. Workers themselves argue that there are insufficient resources or imagination in tackling these challenges of the BME experience in mental health services (Bhui 2002; Evans *et al.* 2006). Acquiescence in the limited potential for change infects the relationship with BME service users. Hopelessness in workers is detected and is highlighted as a major problem by users of mental health services (Office of the Deputy Prime Minister 2004).

Sue Holland (1995) promotes the model of moving from private symptoms to public action. This is an enabling approach that helps users of services to recognise that their experiences are not unique and to join with others to press for changes. This model provides opportunities for workers to demonstrate their support and commitment to advocate for improvements or to support their service users in doing so. Relationships are strengthened through the shared process of tackling challenges.

Speaking about race and racism

Moodley and Palmer (2006) dedicate over 300 pages to exploring how racism can be spoken about in counselling and psychotherapy. Clearly it is not considered to be a straightforward matter. Psychotherapists invest much time in thinking about and learning about human thoughts, feelings and behaviours, including their own. Workers in mental health services struggle with handling race and racism.

It is essential that the deskilling effect of focusing on the obstacles is balanced with attention to the ways of handling race and racism in work with service users. Listening, interviewing and assessment are basic skills but capabilities vary. Many qualitative service user surveys find that service users do not experience staff to be routinely competent in these skills. In the Count Me In inpatient survey 25 per cent of black service users reported that staff never or rarely listen (compared with 11 per cent for all other ethnic groups) (Mental Health Act Commission 2006). Notwithstanding that this study was with admitted patients and that it captures perceptions, as opposed to objective quantitative data the findings are disturbing. A quarter of patients felt that staff whose job it is to specifically listen and support them did not do this. Listening and counselling skills are basic components of the role of front-line professionals. Burnard (2005, p.147) states, 'the attending and listening aspects of counselling are essential aspects that can be used in every health professional's job'.

This level of skill desired by service users from BME backgrounds appears to be beyond the capability of many staff in inpatient mental health services, based on the findings from the inpatient census (Mental Health Act Commission 2006). Organisational factors also have an influence. As Faulkner (1985, p.67) states, 'It is not uncommon for nurses to return to the school after their first ward experience and say "As soon as I tried to talk to patients, someone would ask me to do something else."'

In the context of considerations of ERC good listening requires that attention is paid to the outlook of the service user. The racial identity development grid devised by Sue and Sue (1990) provides a useful framework for considering the way in which people from BME groups see themselves in relation to the white majority (Sue and Sue 1990). The racial identity development grid identifies five stages of development from 'conformity', denoting immersion in the minority culture, to what is described as 'integrative awareness', which is positive regard for both one's own and the majority race and culture. As with all conceptual frameworks this does not enable the categorisation of people where all behaviours comply with a particular type. It does, however, provide a prompt for recognising that there are various forms of racial identity and that therefore there is a need for exploration rather than assumption.

Talking about race and racism will require:

- previous honest dialogue about one's own views and behaviours

- belief that race dialogue is essential if full therapeutic benefit is to be gained from the relationship

- belief that racism has a negative effect on all people of BME groups

- a commitment to tackling both the direct and indirect impacts of racism and discrimination.

Previous honest dialogue about one's own views and behaviours

Discussions about race and racism seem to catch people by surprise. When they are challenged for being racist or for not doing enough for minority groups it evokes emotions ranging from upset to anger. As Bhui (2002, p.122) states, 'antiracist training is often very challenging for participants who find it unbearable to have their integrity questioned'.

The reactions appear to indicate that voicing the accusations is considered to be unjustifiable and unacceptable. Workers who feel that their behaviour is beyond reproach may be affronted that they are accused of being discriminatory, but this does not take into account the fact that the service user may be bringing into the relationship the results of previous experiences. Workers will have emotions and be liable to be hurt and offended but the professional training is designed to enable some acknowledgement of the fact that people will be shaped by their experiences.

Davidson (1985) refers to the development of interpersonal skills in nursing and refers to the process of rehearsing, learning from feedback and applying the learning. Workers who have not undertaken honest exploration of their thoughts and feelings about race, racism and discrimination are likely to be caught out by unanticipated or uncontrolled emotions. Some form of safe open exploration is an absolute prerequisite to relationships that are effective in dealing constructively with matters to do with race, racism and discrimination (Bhugra and Bhui 2001).

Belief that race dialogue is essential if full therapeutic benefit is to be gained from the relationship

Race and racism is not an optional aspect of good mental health care but is central to it. Research findings demonstrate that race makes a difference and that many impacts predate contact with mental health services (Cooper *et al.* 2008; Morgan *et al.* 2005a; Veling *et al.* 2007). It is essential that these issues are considered as core to therapeutic work in mental health. In the same way that it would be a failure to ignore trauma and abuse in mental health, racism and discrimination cannot be ignored.

There are many social and economic factors that have an impact on an individual's recovery. For example, being homeless, unemployed, intoxicated or physically ill will have an impact (Office of the Deputy Prime Minister 2004). The cumulative effect may well undermine resilience (Morgan *et al.* 2005a; Veling *et al.* 2007).

Belief that racism and discrimination have a negative effect on all people from BME backgrounds

All people from BME backgrounds are exposed to the pernicious effects of racism and discrimination. It is well documented that there are ethnic differences in relation to education, housing, employment, experience of the criminal justice system, mental health services and poverty (Commission for Racial Equality 2007; Modood *et al.* 1998). The common theme is that people from many BME groups experience the most undesirable aspects of these socio-economic factors. Workers do, however, sometimes struggle to make sense of disparities in a way that does not locate blame within BME communities.

There has been a re-emergence of discussions about negative psychological effects of slavery that are still being seen (Davis 2007). The impact of racism and discrimination on mental health is well covered in publications (Bhui 2002; Fernando 1991). The extent to which this issue is given prominence is one of the fundamental distinguishing features between paradigms underpinning work with BME groups in mental health. Even the medical profession within mental health does not adopt a view that mental health problems are purely biogenetic (Social Care Institute for Excellence 2007a).

A commitment to tackling both the direct and indirect impacts of racism and discrimination

A major problem for many workers in mental health services is that they feel they are asked to undertake detailed assessment but are then without the means to respond appropriately. There are often barriers to achieving change in the social aspects, such as education, employment and housing. The Care Programme Approach does, however, require that care plans actively tackle these aspects. The review of the implementation of the National Service Framework for Mental Health (Department of Health 2004d) stated that the main focus of the second half of the ten-year programme should be on social inclusion. The establishing of the national programme Delivering Race Equality in mental health was intended to support the progress of the National Service Framework for BME groups. Teams and workers sometimes deal with each case as if it occurs in isolation, but it will strengthen the resolve of workers if they can identify patterns and respond accordingly (see Box 4.1). Statistics may well show that proportionately more BME people on a team's caseload are unemployed or homeless. It would be helpful for this knowledge to influence not only the actions taken for each case but also the collective action by the team. The shift from the individual to the group in tackling systems and authorities is important (Holland 1995). Discussing this approach within direct work with individuals strengthens the ability of the relationship to bring about further positive change. BME service users will be reassured that workers have insight.

How to do it

Insufficient emphasis is given to developing skills through practice. In prequalification and registration for nurses, doctors and social workers practice placements are considered critical, but the approach to skill development in dealing with ERC in mental health services is still training-based rather than competency-based (Bennett *et al.* 2007). The priority should be to have clarity about the end being pursued and to design mechanisms that best achieve these ends. In the field of education, learning and development this is a 'competency-based' model rather than a training-based approach (Bloisi 2006). Delivering Race Equality (Department of Health 2005b) adopts a competency-based approach in the 12 characteristics of future mental heath services. There is, however, difficulty setting out in sufficient detail 'what good looks like' with regard to practice; or in other words, the competencies for effective work with people from BME groups. The work commissioned by the Department of Health Care Services Improvement Partnership on the 'Ten Essential Shared Capabilities' attempts to tackle this (Department of Health 2007b). The 'Ten Essential Shared Capabilities' are those adopted by the Department of Health as being relevant to all working in mental health irrespective of their professional background. They cover capabilities such as working in partnership, promoting recovery and challenging inequality.

Reid and Barrington (1999, p.31) state that, 'learning from life is often superior to learning from theory'. Paying attention to the content of the working relationship with BME service users is largely in the hands of practitioners who are often working alone. A useful way to enable staff to develop is to model the behaviour that they should emulate. Box 5.2 provides some positive examples of direct work between a white mental health worker and BME service users.

Keeping the relationship central is a challenge documented well by Lousada (2000) in his words addressed to psychotherapists:

> It seems to me that we must take seriously the possibility that the caring professions from which we take our recruits are moving towards a state of mind which is to all intents and purposes scared of relationships, of

BOX 5.2 ILLUSTRATION

Community Psychiatric Nurse: Katie

Service User: Carl

Katie: I see from the information you gave us when you came to us six months ago that you used to work as an electrician in your early 20s. It doesn't seem that you've worked since then. Is that correct?

Carl: Yeah. Why?

Katie: I was trying to understand how you feel about it. I know things haven't been that settled for you in the last 12 years but I know sometimes work can help; with money, meeting people and having a routine. That sort of thing.

Carl: I can't work though can I? I'm not really up to it. The medication messes me up real bad. And anyway, no one's going to give me a job.

Katie: I can see why you'd say that but you tell me your reasons for saying no one would give you a job.

Carl: No one wants mad people working for them, do they?

Katie: Don't they? Say more.

Carl: What's your problem? You know how it is. This is pointless...

Katie: In part I was also noticing that you spoke about mental health problems but not about being black. I know that makes a difference too. All the statistics say that black people face a harder time out there in employment and lots of things besides.

Carl: Yeah ... And? ... I'm not interested to be honest. I live with this every day. You been on a training course or something? Have you sorted out the thing with the electricity people? That's what I'm interested in.

Katie: Well, yes. Shall we agree to talk about the electricity first then come back to the other stuff. Agree?

feelings, of being too closely linked to their clients. It is a state of mind that attributes therapeutic benefit to outcome, and not to the relationship which provides the container for it. It is precisely the link between the two that is fractured. (p.477)

Conclusion

There is a dearth of research evidence on what works in reducing disparities for people from BME backgrounds in mental health. The practitioner/ service user relationship as the container for all interventions holds possibilities for finding solutions. There are several obstacles that need to be overcome in building good relationships. Paramount amongst these is a recognition of the need to keep race and racism central in solution-seeking but this must not be at the expense of service users retaining their lead role in care planning.

CHAPTER 6

ETHNICITY IN THE CONTEXT OF OTHER IDENTITIES

People are not one-dimensional. It is important that in giving attention to ERC practitioners do not make assumptions about what is important in a person's identity. There must be a distinction between taking account of the demonstrable impact of discrimination, including racism, and the work on identity. This chapter will consider identity and discrimination against people from BME backgrounds arising from difference in relation to:

- sexuality
- mixed heritage
- BME children brought up in white families or in public care
- gender
- disability.

Sexuality

The concept of specifically named ways of expressing sexuality is a social construction (Greene 2006; Lewis 2006). A result of this social construction is that people recognise that they are defined in a way that is negative if they behave or feel anything other than heterosexual. Gay, lesbian, bisexual and transgender people from BME communities experience a compounding effect of psychological and social discrimination, which is reflected in their experience in mental heath services (Lewis 2006). The psychological impact can be further complicated if, for example, an individual is from a mixed heritage background or in a relationship with someone from a different racial or ethnic background.

White heterosexual mental health workers may feel that they are treading carefully around sensitive matters. Of course, the experiences and backgrounds of workers are more complex. The possible permutations of backgrounds between the worker and the BME service user are numerous. If difference automatically leads to sensitivity and nervousness, the relationships intended to help will be bogged down with avoidance or inadvertent offensiveness.

Sexual expression and sexual identity have been categorised in a way that is sometimes meaningless for the individuals so described. A man who mainly has relationships with women but on occasions has either sex or relationships with men may consider himself as heterosexual or, bisexual or may feel that no description really captures who he is (Department of Health 2007c).

The term 'sexual orientation' has limitations as it conveys only a superficial description of sexual preferences. In fact the identity of a lesbian may well be as much a statement of how she sees herself in relation to men as it is about what she does in the bedroom. This may be representative of a political stance. As such it is important to note that the term 'lesbian' does not describe a homogenous group of women who have sexual relationships with women (Lewis 2006). Against this background it is obvious that current terms such as 'the LGBT agenda' (lesbian, gay, bisexual and transgender) have severe limitations. There is of course a shared agenda in relation to difference and diversity but within the supposed group lie many differences which, if overlooked, will result in a failure to get to the heart of some important issues in mental health services. Women as a group will be considered separately as part of this chapter.

The experiences of people from BME groups who have same-sex relationships need to be considered both in relation to their internal experiences (their identity or the way they see themselves) and discrimination. These will be linked, but the role of mental health services will be different in relation to these. For instance, it may be important to explore with a service user how his or her identity relates to dissonance and stress in a world where heterosexuality is presented as the norm. In relation to making referrals or dealing with group situations it may be necessary for a worker to take on a role in challenging discrimination, where this is known to exist. Further still, a worker may need to be alert to where discrimination is more covert than verbal or physical assaults.

People from sexual minority communities have different and poorer experiences of mental health services (David and Knight 2008; King *et al.* 2003; Razzano *et al.* 2006). For people from BME groups these issues are compounded as a result of the multiple effects of having several minority identities (Jackson and Brown 1996; Mind 2007).

Mental health workers need to have some awareness of the possible experiences of people from BME backgrounds who are lesbian, gay, bisexual or transgender, or who do not have sexual relationships exclusively with people of the opposite sex. This awareness should not lead the worker to make assumptions or relentlessly to pursue a subject that may be regarded as a personal and private matter by the service user (King *et al.* 2003). Knowledge and awareness can, however, prevent assumptions being made (e.g. that people are heterosexual) and will enable informed exploration of the service user's feelings and experiences.

Feelings and experiences of people from BME groups who are from sexual minorities and who use mental health services – what workers should know

These points do not relate to all people but are sufficiently common to be taken into account by workers.

BOX 6.1 FEELINGS

In relation to the majority within their own ethnic group, people from BME groups who are also part of a sexual minority sometimes feel:

- they are in conflict with their ethnic group
- shame, in relation to their ethnic group
- multiple aspects of their identity are shameful or weak
- anger, because they experience the most hostile treatment from people within their own ethnic group
- at risk of a sharper type of hostility.

(David and Knight 2008; Ingram 1999; Jackson and Brown 1996; Lewis 2006)

Personal feelings projected onto white workers:

- they are making things worse for themselves
- multiple aspects of their identity are problems
- an unwillingness to be open about their sexual identity to avoid betraying their ethnic community (irrespective of whether they really feel part of any such community).

Generally they may feel:

- they have too many issues
- they are not understood fully by any minority group – and that in different contexts either their identity as a service user, someone from a BME group or someone from a sexual minority has to be suppressed or disregarded
- they are unlikely ever to have an intimate relationship as a result of both of the above.

(Elze 2002; Jackson and Brown 1996; Lewis 2006)

People from both BME and sexual minority backgrounds will have particular experiences irrespective of whether they are open about their sexual identity. See Box 6.2.

BOX 6.2 EXPERIENCES

People from both BME and sexual minority backgrounds may experience:

- greater hostility from their own ethnic group
- their sexuality being challenged by staff from religious or faith groups who feel that this is something their belief obliges them to do
- mental health staff from the same BME group speaking inappropriately and discriminating as though a common ethnic identity legitimises this
- being verbally attacked, including being accused of becoming like white people, bringing shame on the community and being responsible for spreading AIDs
- victims of assault, which is more common for sexual minority groups
- left unprotected when other service users make discriminatory comments.

This list is compiled from reports made directly to the author as well as studies by Ingram 1999; Jackson and Brown 1996; King et al. 2003; Lewis 2006.

What BME sexual minorities feel and what they express may be different. This does not give licence for disregarding what people say on the assumption that they are not expressing their true feelings. Knowledge of possible feelings and experiences can equip mental health workers to open a conversation, where there appears to be a split between what is said and how the service user behaves. A role of the worker is to help reduce this dissonance where possible. There appears to be a causal link between the negative feelings and experiences identified in Boxes 6.1 and 6.2, and mental health problems.

Impacts of negative experiences on mental health

The development of sexual identity is complex and there is no single theory on why some people are heterosexual and some are not, or why some people have both gay and heterosexual relationships (Konik and Stewart 2004). It is important, however, to recognise that the factors that ultimately lead to use of mental health services are unlikely to be related to a single aspect of an individual's life. Practitioners should not thoughtlessly construct a theory of sexual identity development that brands anything other than heterosexuality as an abnormality. Hellman and Klein (2004) identify the error in this paradigm when they state that many people have a belief that homosexuality occurs in troubled heterosexuals.

One likely effect on some mental health workers of considering the feelings and experiences of sexual minorities is that it will highlight their own discomfort about these issues. For some workers it will provoke outright objections to the suggestion that anything other than heterosexual practices or relationships are normal and acceptable. The development of the competence of mental health workers tends to focus primarily on practice and behaviours, not beliefs. It is common, however, for beliefs that are held strongly to emerge inadvertently. It is imperative that workers honestly consider their own beliefs, thoughts and feelings. Workers need to be honest about where they identify conflicts with what is required by law and policy, and they need to find ways reduce or eliminate these conflicts. The Equalities Act (2006) makes it illegal to discriminate against people on the basis of their sexuality. It is likely, however, that an attempt to comply with legislation and policy in a way that is void of empathy will lead to poor practice (Mearns and Thorne 1988).

Mental health workers must, above all, strive to maintain the physical and psychological safety of all service users. A failure to tackle verbal or physical aggression towards sexual minorities is a breach of a fundamental duty. Workers who themselves perpetrate harassment, whatever their motivation, place themselves at serious risk of disciplinary action if their organisation deals with these matters seriously. As a minimum they may be required to undertake development work that enables them to be fit to practice.

Bearing in mind a service user's possible feelings and experiences as a result of being from a sexual minority, it is difficult to justify a worker's failure to discuss this in the therapeutic relationship. It is imperative that eagerness to explore these issues does not lead to over-emphasis on something that is not considered to be problematic.

Asking about sexual orientation is not straightforward. Many workers experience it as tantamount to asking people about how they have sex. In fact, asking about sexual orientation can be about relationships and identity. In 2007 the Healthcare Commission introduced a question about sexual orientation in the inpatient census 'Count Me In'. On the last day in March workers in inpatient settings in the NHS and independent psychiatric hospitals had to ask a range of questions and compile and submit data for everyone admitted at the time. When it was first proposed that sexual orientation should be included in the dataset many respondents to the Healthcare Commission argued that this would be intrusive. In addition many were convinced that there would be very little useful data gained as most patients would choose not to answer the question. In 2007, 82 per cent of the 30,804 records for people aged 16 and over submitted included a categorisation for sexual orientation. Of these, 1 per cent responded that they were gay/lesbian, and 1 per cent bisexual; less than 1 per cent said 'other' and 9 per cent said 'prefer not to say'. Sixteen per cent of records showed 'not known' and 2 per cent were not valid returns for this question. In the cohort of 16 per cent of records that showed 'not known' for sexual orientation this will have included a number of responses where sexual orientation was not asked (Commission for Healthcare Audit and Inspection 2007a). The Commission for Healthcare Audit and Inspection point out that 127 providers submitted returns that included no patient coded as being gay, lesbian or bisexual. The commission postulated that this indicates that 'not known' cohort almost certainly includes people who are gay, lesbian or bisexual meaning that percentages recorded for these groups do not fully reflect the numbers in services and in particular, those who would be prepared to disclose this.

The increased openness in society about difference should not be interpreted by the practitioner as signifying that service users will have fewer negative experiences or complications of identity. Workers should on the contrary feel more confident in fulfilling their role in relation to exploring issues that may be relevant in the mental health issues of the service user.

How to ask about sexual identity

The problem with asking about sexual identity resides in the feeling and fears of the workers. These often arise from:

- a misunderstanding about what is being asked – i.e. about identity, not sexual practices

- a belief that it is unnecessarily intrusive

- a belief that they do not have the right to ask

- a lack of awareness about the potential importance of the issue

- an unconscious fear or uncertainty about their own sexuality

- previous experiences of someone objecting to being asked

- their own objection to being asked.

WHY ASK?

The first stage in developing confidence to ask is to discuss and explore the reasons for asking. The content of this chapter demonstrates that people from BME groups who are from a sexual minority are at greater risk of internal and external negative experiences and that these are potentially detrimental to good mental health. King *et al.* (2003, p.7) make the recommendation, 'Health and social services agencies should monitor the particular experiences and satisfaction levels of LGB people as users of services, and put in place, mechanisms to respond to feedback.'

WHAT TO ASK

A risk in modern mental health services is that in order to manage anxieties at practitioner, senior manager or political levels approaches become increasingly formulaic. Workers may be asked to, or may be inclined to stick rigidly to asking set questions. In doing so they may show disregard for the uniqueness of their service user/worker relationship. Most workers would appreciate that it would be helpful to have an idea of what kinds of relationships service users find fulfilling. This is a legitimate area of professional curiosity, or in other words, part of the assessment. A worker should therefore consider asking about relationships or identity. Being confident about the reason for asking will enable the worker either to offer an explanation by way of introduction or to respond to questions about the relevance of the particular line of questioning. See Box 6.3 for examples. This material can be covered in assessments for new clients or as a new area being explored in an existing relationship with a service user. King *et al.* (2003, p.7) also recommend, in particular professionals will need to strike a balance between the extremes of:

- *regarding same sex attraction as the underlying cause of psychological difficulties*

- *ignoring sexuality altogether*

- *displaying excessive curiosity about how LGB people live.*

Mixed heritage

There is no single ethnic group described as 'mixed race' (Robinson 2005). It does not take a moment to imagine the unfathomable number of potential racial or ethnic combinations of parents. Mixed ethnic identities can be even more unfathomable when it is considered that either one or both parents may themselves feel they have a mixed identity. If this sense of identity is passed on it is possible that offspring will feel ethnically mixed in a way that does not lend itself to ticking from a list of preset categorisations.

The themes in this book are relevant to all people who are from a black or minority ethnic background. Evidence suggests that within the context of the poor experience of BME people in mental health services, people from some categories of mixed heritage are having dramatically poorer experiences (Mental Health Act Commission 2006, 2008). Knowledge of mixed heritage identity, and the internal and external experience of this, are important in understanding the relationship with poorer mental health service utilisation and outcomes. Certain themes run through studies that look at mixed heritage:

- complexities in identity development

- parental ambivalence about ethnic identity

- family conflict (perhaps suppressed)

- dislocation within society

- overlooked identity.

(Katz 1996; Okitikpi 2005a; Tizard and Phoenix 1993)

Identity development

Banks (2002a) and Katz (1996) provide useful overviews of identity development generally and specifically in relation to being of mixed heritage.

BOX 6.3 ILLUSTRATION

Examples of approaches to questioning:
'Some of the service users (or clients or patients) with whom I work identify themselves as gay, lesbian, bisexual, transgender or prefer no label but would not see themselves as heterosexual. Research demonstrates that certain people have a harder time both in society and in mental health services and this has a negative impact on their mental health. If there are aspects of your experiences that add to the risks of you having or maintaining good mental health it may be helpful if we discuss them so that we can jointly consider ways to deal with any problems or concerns. How would *you* identify yourself?'

'I'm aware that people find closeness and intimacy in different kinds of relationships and depending on the nature of these (whether they are same sex or with the opposite sex) people feel differently about themselves and often are treated differently. Research tells us that these differences do have an impact on mental health so I wondered if you feel that your sexual identity raised any particular issues in your life? How would you describe your sexual orientation/identity?'

'Our organisation has started monitoring sexual orientation to help ensure that we respond fairly to the particular needs that people have. We know that unless we know about people's sexual orientation we can't take this into account whether on an individual level or at an organisational level. Do you mind describing how you see your sexual orientation? One option is to decline to answer and no assumptions are made about this. We have people of all different orientations who just feel that it is not relevant and just decline. As I said, research indicates that it is relevant but you must feel free to respond in a way that makes sense to you.'

'I'm interested in finding out aspects of your experience which have either caused distress, perhaps through discrimination or social stigma, or have enhanced the quality of your life – as such I wonder whether you would feel comfortable telling me about your romantic life?'

'How would you describe your sexual orientation?'

The process involves identifying with one or both racial groups and moving through stages of acceptance and, it is hoped, positive regard. On this journey individuals may immerse themselves in or reject one or other of their racial heritages.

The language in the Western world emphasises opposites. With regard to race Okitikpi (2005b) refers to a binary world. People of mixed heritage are, in these terms, neither one race nor another. This way of seeing people becomes internalised for individuals of mixed heritage. The feeling of not having a distinct ethnic or racial identity can affect self-esteem (Robinson 2005). Katz (1996) and Tizard and Phoenix (1993), however, state that it is a myth that people of mixed heritage suffer more problems with self-esteem than black people. There are differences between groups of mixed heritage. Where the sense of opposites is greater in the racial background of parents, the mixed racial identity holds more conflict. People of black and white mixed heritage are often described as being caught in the middle because of the legacy of international and national racial conflicts. The national inpatient census report emphasises the disparities for people of black mixed heritage in both the quantitative and qualitative findings (Mental Health Act Commission 2006).

Notwithstanding the fact that identity is comprised of much more than ethnicity or race, people of mixed heritage are sometimes referred to as the embodiment of conflict. Where a conflict between black and white people arises, they are asked to make a choice, this requirement often coming from themselves as much as other people. The effect of this is that people of mixed heritage can in effect be asked to choose one parent over another or to deny or deride one aspect of their racial identity (Okitikpi 1999). These internal tensions become more intrusive if individuals' physical appearance would indicate that they are closer to one racial group but they do not feel this; worse still, they may feel strongly allied to the other racial group. Some black and white mixed race people with darker skin are treated as if they are black (Tizard and Phoenix 1993; Zeitlin 2002). They are told that it is a well-established fact that if they have any black blood (meaning heritage) then they are automatically considered as black. This of course was the approach taken in overtly racist regimes (Owusu-Bempah 2005). For some people of mixed heritage this assumption of blackness is problematic because they may in fact feel negative towards black people as a result of a form of internalised racism (Fanon 1967). This may arise from a range of factors such as a negative experience of an absent parent, hostility or rejection from black groups (where they may have believed they would find allies).

There are many permutations to the internal conflicts that can arise. The relationship with one or both parents, whether they are absent, present, primary carer or not, can add to the problems. The belief that races are fixed biological categories is the source of many of the problems that impinge upon people of mixed heritage. The flaws in this conceptualisation of race were discussed in Chapter 1. Katz (1996) comments on the undue emphasis placed upon biogenetic concepts for legitimising the division of humanity along racial lines.

Parental ambivalence

A parent who has a child with a partner of a different racial background may have various feelings about seeing his or her offspring as belonging to a different group (Banks 2002b). This discussion does not disregard the positive maternal or paternal feelings that are likely to be a feature of raising a child. There are, however, many contexts when the difference is highlighted and this has an impact on the relationship between parent and child. For example, a black parent who takes his or her child of mixed heritage to the country of the parent's heritage may heighten the child's feelings of being outside the group, or a child may hear or observe a parent being racist and feel rejected.

The most commonly discussed parent/child relationship is that of the white mother and the child of mixed heritage, where there is an absent father. Banks (2002b) discussed the notion of the psychological trap, where a woman may feel that her options for a new partner are limited because she has a child of mixed heritage. This can in turn leave the child feeling that he or she is unwanted baggage.

The feelings that arise from being of mixed heritage in situations of parental ambivalence are often not spoken about. In part, people of mixed heritage will feel limited in the network of people with whom they could discuss such issues. Siblings may produce an empathic ear but not necessarily so. Other people of mixed heritage, for example at school or at a club, may not be the kind of people with whom a natural friendship would blossom. It is often the case that these feelings and thoughts are hardly expressed, if ever at all. The impacts of these feelings, however, are not always so easily ignored.

Family conflict

The impact of discord in a family of mixed heritage potentially brings racial difference to the fore (Banks 2002b). Where statements are made about an individual parent but these sound like a racial stereotype or slur, this raises anxieties about race and racism but seldom would this be discussed. A child of mixed heritage could therefore live with a contradiction of parents who supposedly at some stage (if not still) experienced love but where there is nevertheless racial tension. There are many potential situations when race can become an unspoken 'elephant in the room'.

Dislocation within society

People of mixed heritage are not seen as having a racial identity in their own right. There is not a single line of heritage, a notional homeland of the race. There is often a sense of not belonging but falling between racial groups (Owusu-Bempah 2005). A consequence is that people of mixed heritage live in a society where they may feel no natural kinship, apart from with people who feel similarly. Tizard and Phoenix (1993) do, however, make the point that young people of mixed heritage do utilise various protective strategies for dealing with racism, such as developing a strong sense of identity.

Overlooked identity

Until relatively recently reports on health and social care or education, for example, would discuss people from minority ethnic groups and ignore people of mixed heritage. People of mixed heritage are sometimes left feeling as though even in formal publications an assumption is made that they are black, though this has been changing in recent years (Okitikpi 2005a).

Relationship with mental health problems

The statistics on the experience of people from mixed heritage backgrounds in mental health services are limited because it is only recently that this group has been recognised in its own right. There have been few specific studies but the 2005 inpatient 'Count Me In' census did reveal that people of mixed heritage reported poor experiences (Mental Health Act Commission 2006). People of 'mixed ethnicity' comprised 10 per cent of the sample of 394 patients who reported their ethnicity in the follow-up interviews to the census. Compared with the entire cohort they:

- were referred less frequently for cognitive behavioural therapy (CBT) – (5% compared with 14% for 'All')

- reported that nursing staff were rarely or never polite – (13% compared with 7% generally)

- said they were rarely or never treated fairly – (20% compared with 13% generally)

- said that psychiatrists were rarely or never friendly – (18% compared with 10% in the 'All' category).

In relation to the final point, people in the 'mixed ethnicity' category reported the greatest degree of difference. In other cases there were other groups that showed a greater degree of variation but the 'mixed ethnicity' category was not far behind (Mental Health Act Commission 2006).

The proportion of patients from mixed backgrounds in each 'Count Me In' census since its inception in 2005 has been notable. Of the 32,000 patients surveyed in 2007, 2.1 per cent were from a mixed race background; the same as people identified as 'African' (Commission for Healthcare Audit and Inspection 2007a).

There are many potential stressors in the lives of people of mixed heritage. Front-line workers should be interested in the specific ethnic identity of the people with whom they are working. A skilled worker who provides a safe context to explore issues arising from mixed heritage identity may be affording a service user a rare opportunity to articulate honestly concerns that act as unspoken stressors.

BME children brought up in white families or in public care

This section relates to the experience of mental health problems and services as a result of:

- identity issues in relation to having the physical features of someone from a particular ethnic group but having no natural affinity to, or knowledge of this group

- ambivalent relationships with white parental figures.

Data have consistently shown that a disproportionately high number of children from BME groups are taken into the 'Looked After System' ('in care'), particularly African Caribbean children (Mehra 2002; Zeitlin 2002). Of the children being looked after on 31 March 2005, 8 per cent were from a mixed heritage background against a 8 per cent representation in the general population. The figures are identical for children of African Caribbean backgrounds. Of the children placed for adoption in the year to 31 March 2005, children of mixed heritage represented over twice the percentage of all other BME groups together (Department for Education and Skills 2006). Studies show that of all the children from BME backgrounds who are adopted, fostered or in residential care, few are racially matched (Mehra 2002; Zeitlin 2002).

The impact on identity

Not all white adoptive parents or foster carers fail to respond to the need to develop a positive sense of ethnic identity and heritage of the BME children in their care. Evidence suggests, however, that there are many BME children who do not have their needs met (Okitikpi 1999; Tizard and Phoenix 1993). This relates not only to having information about their ethnic group and contact with people from a similar background who are culturally secure. Zeitlin (2002) wisely makes the distinction between race (physical attributes) and culture in this context. He points out that studies consistently show that in terms of educational and social outcomes, BME young people brought up in care do no worse than others. The assumed link between a strong ethnic identity and self-esteem, he argues, is unfounded. It is well accepted however, that there are consequences in relation to disconnection from cultural heritage and also the limits in relation to helping BME young people develop strategies for dealing with racism and discrimination (Davis 2007; Mehra 2002; Tizard and Phoenix 1993; Zeitlin 2002). BME children who find themselves in the situation of having white parental figures need to have a context in which they can be open about the issues this raises for them. Most typically these feelings are triggered when the reality of their situation is reflected back to them, for example when they are out in public as a family unit. The things that children feel other people think about them may be real (based on how people behave) or they may be the projections of their own feelings. Whatever the reality in any given situation, the feelings, whether current or not, need to be explored.

Empathy can only arise from some appreciation of the thoughts and feelings of the other (Lawrence et al. 2004). A mental health worker will benefit from knowing that it is likely that someone from a BME group with experiences such as those described here may have complex feelings about his or her racial or ethnic identity (Thoburn 2005). The relevance of this is not only in relation to understanding potential contributory factors to current mental health problems; the knowledge will inform the assessments and equip the worker to open up discussions in this area. Usually an inherited file will have a record of the person's history. If this information is not available it will probably emerge during an assessment as personal history is gathered. However, unless a worker is mindful of the potential implications of the information about a transracial adoption or long-term foster placement the only purpose it will serve is to enable services to hold a tidy chronology.

Implications for practice

Looked after children are more likely to use mental health services (McAuley and Young 2006). Many issues of identity discussed in relation to children of mixed heritage apply here. An important aspect to consider for people who have been in long-term care is the extent to which a worker may make assumptions, based on physical attributes, about what constitutes their ethnic identity.

The concept of the 'hierarchy of blackness' (or Asian-ness, etc.) is well established in minority communities though the phrase itself may not be. This is an unspoken ascription of superiority to people and behaviours seen as more clearly accentuating ethnic pride and tradition. Fanon (1967) discusses the ways in which black people attempt to protect themselves from racial rejection by adopting what he refers to as a 'white mask'. This has the consequence of creating a 'disconnect' from the minority community of which the person is apparently a part (Davis 2007). This broken connection can evoke a desire in an individual to avoid contact with his or her own group.

The criteria for acceptance within a group are not fixed either in time, place or concept (Hall 1996). Having a white partner, liking rock music and fish and chips, and speaking with a middle-class accent may be factors that lead to a sense of being on the outside of a minority group. This is not fixed. The views of working-class African Caribbean teenagers about what constitutes blackness will be different to those of a group of black film makers, academics or artists considered as radical in their circles.

There are signifiers of belonging to a racial or ethnic group, which can cause exclusion either by self or others, and within the group there are subcultures and groupings that push this further (Hall 1996). The feeling of not fitting in, not knowing the norms or not feeling at home with the group is accentuated for BME people who may have had limited positive exposure to the things that are considered in society to be cultural norms for the groups to which they belong. Workers therefore need to be thoughtful when they offer services described as ethnic or culturally specific. The desire to address racial, ethnic or cultural needs could lead to insensitivity and stressful feelings on the part of the service user. Workers may experience an antagonistic response as a defence against uncomfortable feelings.

The handling of these matters is improved where workers not only gather information, such as a history of being looked after or adopted, but where they consider the implications. Conversations about difficult aspects may evoke reactions that are difficult to deal with. Mental health services generally see their role as maintaining order and calm. In psychological therapies it is more common to expect that by dealing with painful subjects there will potentially be a period of distress but that this is the pathway to recovery and healing (Mearns and Thorne 1988).

Gender

Gender relates to the socially determined aspects of the characteristics of men and women; this is different to 'sex' which refers to the biological differences (Canales 2000). This distinction is important because it denotes the source of many of the differences between men and women that are commonly experienced and observed. Most differences arise from the differences in the way boys and girls are raised and responded to in society. This creates a cyclical effect of socialisation in families and societies (Canales 2000). The differences are profound; there is inequality and inequity and as a group women are seriously damaged and undermined by these factors. All too often these involve violence and subjugation. Although this consideration of gender will cover briefly some issues pertinent to men from BME backgrounds, the main focus will be on the needs of women.

There are differences in the experiences of women and men in mental health services (Scheyett and McCarthy 2006). Ethnicity adds another dimension and the experience of women from BME groups in relation to mental health and the use of services is worthy of attention. Government policy gave a focus to the mental health needs of women in 2002 with the publication of the consultation document *Women's Mental Health: Into the Mainstream* (Department of Health 2002a). It is noticeable, however, when reading this implementation guidance that the relationship between ethnicity, gender and mental health is not salient. This reflects the general fact that researchers and writers often find it difficult to express the relationship between characteristics of an individual's identity and experiences. The compounding effect of gender and ethnicity is a significant concern to many, as was evident from the feedback on the consultation on the emerging implementation guidance (2003a). This guidance was published later that year entitled *Mainstreaming Gender and Mental Health*. (Department of Health 2003b).

Women generally have poorer experiences within and outside the mental health system. Many of these would, even to a layperson, be obvious contributors to poor, rather than good mental health. Women are more likely to:

- be victims of child sexual abuse
- be the victims of domestic violence

- have experienced some form of sexual violence

- be lone parents or primary carers

- be unemployed and suffering social and economic hardship

- express their distress in physical self-harm.

(Department of Health 2003b)

The experiences of women from BME groups who use mental health services are more negative within and outside of the system. There are significant differences according to ethnic group but there are common themes. In comparison with white women, those from BME groups are more likely to:

- experience language barriers

- be lone parents or primary carers

- be unemployed and suffering social and economic hardship

- have their child placed in public care.

(Canales 2000; Chantler 2002; Department of Health 2003b)

And specifically in the mental health system are:

- more likely to receive a diagnosis for a psychotic disorder

- more likely to be in a locked environment

- more likely to be victims of harassment

- less likely to receive taking therapies.

(Commission for Healthcare Audit and Inspection 2007a;
Mental Health Act Commission 2006; Raleigh *et al.* 2007)

Women from BME groups are the most disadvantaged within two already disadvantaged groups. There are many potential ways that these differences may be manifested. A woman from a BME group who has limited English will be more reliant on others to enable communication. This may lead to poor practice where unqualified interpreters are used, for example a male partner (Chantler 2002). This creates a conflict if part of the problem experienced by the service user relates to the power dynamic within that relationship. It may be one in which she is socially and financially reliant on the man and this may lead to a context where emotional or physical abuse is accepted because of a feeling of having no options. This abuse is highly unlikely to emerge in an assessment if the perpetrator is acting as the interpreter.

Asylum seekers, refugees and trauma

Though immigration status is not an aspect of ethnicity there is a clear relationship between the two. Women who are either asylum seekers or refugees are likely to have experienced horrific traumatic events (Silove *et al.* 1997). These experiences are likely to create ambivalent relationships with men, who are often the perpetrators of such crimes. There may be physical health problems arising from their experiences and there are almost certainly going to be emotional and psychological consequences which would be fundamental to any understanding of the needs of a woman who may end up using mental health services. Mental health workers will need to ensure that they are equipped at least to assess whether specialist trauma support is required. Failure to take these issues into account when making an assessment and delivering services could easily be experienced as further abuse (Tribe 1999). For someone previously detained and tortured it is likely to be an intensely negative experience to be detained in hospital.

Workers in mental health services need to be mindful of the types of issues highlighted above and ensure that assessment and practice take these into account. As with other aspects of identity, the impacts of gender and ethnicity should be explored within the relationship with service users. Some of the responses that are required will be beyond the knowledge or capability of front-line workers. For example, alternative arrangements may be required for the provision of interpreting services or post-trauma services.

Front-line workers have a role in helping women to organise and create their own collective voice. Sue Holland (1995) presents the model of moving from private symptoms to social action. The power of collective action is important for any group trying to effect change. For women from BME groups this is important because one of the consequences of the cumulative negative experiences is the increased likelihood of poor self-esteem and isolation. The underlying message in many characterisations of women is that they are to blame for the situation in which they find themselves. This relates to both the way a specific individual may be perceived and treated as well as the language used about women in general (Canales 2000). Mental health workers need to maintain a constant check on their own language and behaviours to determine whether they are falling into the default position of society's perception and portrayal of women. It is important for mental health practitioners to be clear about what is being done in relation to four responsibilities:

- ensuring that women are not discriminated against in their own practice
- ensuring that assessments and care plans are appropriate and responsive
- challenging discrimination in other people and organisations
- advocating for women, for example in relation to service development.

These responsibilities are the mainstay of the role of an effective practitioner in relation to any service user. The necessity to consider the specific needs of BME women is compromised because of the routine social interactions between men and women on a daily basis. Society functions on the basis of a superficial sense of harmony between the sexes, despite regular emergence of difference and hierarchy (Banton 1965). A worker needs to be able to constantly assess the potential impact of being a woman from a BME group on the relationship and on the service user's experiences, and to be responsive to these.

The gender/ethnicity capable practitioner checklist

The four key responsibilities of practitioners listed above are explored through a set of questions. These may serve as an internal check for any worker seeking to ensure that he or she demonstrates the capabilities required.

BOX 6.4 THE GENDER/ETHNICITY CAPABLE PRACTITIONER CHECKLIST

Ensuring that I do not discriminate against women in my own practice
- Am I aware of the stereotypes people have of women from different ethnic groups?
- What are my personal views about how I believe a woman should speak or act?
- Do I behave in ways that perpetuate stereotypes?
- Have I asked whether there is anything in relation to gender or ethnicity that I should be aware of and take into account in the relationship?

Ensuring that assessments and care plans are appropriate and responsive

- Does the assessment that I undertook with the service user include considerations of the impact of being a woman from a BME group?
- Have I asked about whether there have been experiences of the abuse; whether physical, emotional or sexual?
- Have I supported the service user to feel comfortable when expressing preferences based on her gender and ethnicity (including religion)?
- Do the assessment and care plan include any arrangements for providing access to ethnic- or gender-specific services?

Challenging discrimination in other people and organisations

- Have I been alert to language that may belie discriminatory views when I have received referrals?
- Have my onward referrals received a response that indicates that discriminatory views will influence the outcome?
- Did the assessment, care plan or any aspect of the work raise previous or current experiences of discrimination by any person or organisation? Have I raised this with them as an area of concern or something for which redress is being sought?

Advocating for women, for example in relation to service development

- Do I see myself as having a role in advocating for the closure of any gaps in service provision for women?
- Have I highlighted to my manager or anyone else with authority any difficulties in helping to meet the needs of women through available resources (services, networks or finances to enable access to support)?
- Do I know who is responsible for ensuring that the organisation's Gender Equality Scheme is implemented?
- Do I know if we have a specific women's strategy and/or action plan? Do I use and support the authority that already exists?

Box 6.5 provides an illustration of a male worker who had internalised the gender/ethnicity capable checklist.

BOX 6.5 ILLUSTRATION

Simon is a social worker in a mental health team on the outskirts of Manchester. He is working with Paulette, a woman from Dominica in the Caribbean. She is 46 years old and has been in England for 27 years. She has a diagnosis of bipolar affective disorder. She has been in the psychiatric system since she was 25 years old. Her baby son was then three and a half years old and the father had recently died in a workplace accident.

Having had a period of relative stability Paulette's mental health deteriorated recently. The most striking change in her life was that her son, now aged 24, had been to Dominica and came back speaking and behaving very much as if he identified with being Dominican rather than being British, though it was his first ever trip there. Paulette appeared at first to be jubilant about her son's new-found ethnic pride but then over a period of weeks she became subdued. She began to withdraw from contact with her friends and people from the church, where much of her social life centred.

Simon spent a long time (over a series of visits) speaking with Paulette and making connections. It transpired that her late husband was also Dominican and was in his mid-20s when he died. Her son's new Dominican persona had made her dwell on the experiences and isolation that she had undergone 21 years previously. In the years that followed the death of her husband she entered into a series of relationships with men that were shallow by choice but which also often ended up being abusive. Looking back she feels that she was raped on more than one occasion. At the time she was, in her own words, 'trying to enjoy life' and felt she had little by way of rights and self-esteem. Her feelings of shame about her life in her 20s were mixed with outrage at the way she was treated by men who she felt took advantage of her. She longed for the sense she had back then, of feeling 'Dominican and proud' but would have liked to have forgotten the grimness of isolation and abuse she experienced.

Simon's approach
Simon is white. He wanted to ensure that Paulette was not discriminated against in his own practice. He therefore:

- reflected on whether he harboured any unhelpful stereotypes about black women and promiscuity
- considered whether he felt any different about acceptable sexual behaviour of men and women
- tried to understand what it meant to Paulette to be Dominican. He tried to understand the impact of it being a former French colony and the impact of the language and cultural differences between this and other Caribbean islands
- asked how Paulette felt about talking with him about her experiences and about her ethnic identity. He asked whether there was anything important to her that he could take account of.

Simon tried to ensure that assessments and care plans were appropriate and responsive. He therefore:

- asked Paulette about how she would like to try to move though this stage of her life
- spoke about different ways she could get help
- asked whether, given the things that were emerging for her, she wished to have a different care coordinator, bearing in mind that he was white and male
- asked about any support she had received in the past in relation to the experiences of abuse and whether there was: a) any specific service support that she wanted and b) any action she wanted to take in relation to the crimes committed against her 20 years earlier
- discussed counselling and the potential for access to a service that had ethnic and racial identity and the needs of women as central considerations
- discussed how she might have access to a service or community group that enabled her to have positive experiences of celebrating her heritage. Simon asked a community worker to help him investigate whether there were any specific Dominican community groups locally. He asked whether Paulette felt that she would like to try to save and visit Dominica.

Simon felt that it was part of his role to challenge discrimination in other people and organisations. He therefore:

- spoke with the previous care coordinator (who had moved to work in an early intervention service in the same NHS Trust) and explained that previous summaries stated that Paulette's cultural needs were met through her networks at church. The Baptist church that Paulette attended had over 160 regular members, only three of whom were black. Paulette was the only one with a Dominican heritage. Simon said that it seemed as if stereotypical assumptions had been made by the previous worker.

- challenged his manager who had reprimanded him for offering Paulette the option of changing her care co-ordinator. He said he accepted that it would have been helpful to have discussed it with his manager first but he said that it was unacceptable for her to say (as she had done) that she 'would not even think about it, never in a million years'. He said that such a closed mind in the context of legitimate considerations was discriminatory whether intended or not.

Simon knew he had a role in advocating for women and people from BME groups. He therefore:

- asked his manager if they could have a discussion in the team meeting about Paulette, using her case to think through how they deal with allocation of cases when new information emerges
- spoke with the person in Trust headquarters who had responsibility for equalities and asked about the work that was happening to improve services for women and people from BME groups
- made recommendations to the Trust's lead on women and to the Learning and Development Department about the need for more support for teams and individuals on working with women who have experienced sexual abuse.

Men

The systems in mental health services reflect the power dynamics in society. They are more geared to meet the needs of men. There are, however, some specific needs of men from BME backgrounds in mental health services. Research studies have shown that men are:

- less likely to seek help for their mental or emotional distress
- less likely to confide in a friend
- more likely to enter the mental health system through aversive routes

- more likely to receive the more restrictive interventions of mental health services such as physical restraint and seclusion

- more likely to be admitted to intensive care units and secure facilities

- less likely to receive talking therapies

- most likely to die of suicide than any other cause if they are aged under 35.

(Addis and Mahalik 2003; Canales 2000; Commission for Healthcare Audit and Inspection 2007a; Department of Health 2002b; Griffiths 1992)

These general patterns are true for men from BME backgrounds. The most extreme variations relate to men from African and African Caribbean (black) backgrounds.

Men from black backgrounds (compared with white men):

- are more frequently admitted via the criminal justice system

- experience greater use of seclusion

- stay longer in the facilities

- are less likely to be referred for talking therapies.

(Commission for Healthcare Audit and Inspection 2007a, b)

It is important for mental health workers to be mindful of these patterns and to consider whether in their own practice they conform to stereotyping. Practitioners need to evaluate whether there are any assumptions underpinning the support being considered or offered to men. Without conscious consideration it may be that a worker will less readily refer a man for therapy. Services need to move away from acting according to default positions and towards assessing and responding to the unique needs of individuals and keeping all possibilities in mind.

Disability

There are many forms of disability that may that may have an impact on experience or identity. Not only will the specific nature of the disability have an impact but also the age at which this occurred. Public authorities are required under the Disability Discrimination Act (2005) to set out how they will promote equality for disabled people, in Disability Equality Schemes.

Some people argue that rather than seeing people as having disabilities, a preferred conceptualisation is that people are disabled by the actions or omissions of others. An impairment is the attribute or feature within the person (Morris 2004a). Being disabled can be seen as representing more than a physical or mental hurdle but also a political one. The location of the 'problem' is the determinant of the social conceptualisation of disability.

As with other issues covered in this chapter, being disabled can represent an aspect of personal identity that is celebrated rather than borne begrudgingly.

Mental health workers need to utilise good listening and interviewing skills to ascertain from service users how they see their identity. Different aspects of their identity may have centrality at different times (Jones *et al.* 2007). Identity is clearly not fixed and certain aspects will be more salient or defining depending on circumstances. People from BME groups who have mental health problems and who are disabled will have multiple identities (Ahmad 2000; Morris 2004a). A more accurate description may be that they will have an identity comprised of many facets.

Modern mental health services seek to tackle social exclusion and discrimination and this requires workers to move beyond the narrow considerations of 'symptoms' to a recognition of the needs of the whole person. In keeping with the view that people are disabled by the actions of others, mental health workers need to check their own practice to see if they act in ways that are unlawfully discriminatory. Workers also need to consider in the lives of the service users they work with whether any other individual or agency acts in a way that disadvantages a disabled service user. In such cases it is a central part of the role of the worker to challenge this.

A consequence of being from a BME group and being disabled is that interactions with other people hold so many possibilities for discrimination (Rubino 2001). This can range from actions that are stigmatising to overt discrimination such as preventing access and inclusion. Where there are other aspects of identity such as being a woman or being gay, lesbian, bisexual or transgender the world holds a multitude of possible hostilities (Morris 2004b). This is not restricted to a nebulous 'society'. Friends, family and colleagues can drive people to isolation through deliberate or inadvertent acts of discrimination. Workers need to be mindful that they are probably not beginning a relationship with a disabled BME service user from a position of neutrality. The service user's experiences to date are likely to set an expectation that in one way or another the worker is going to say or do something that fails to respond appropriately to his or her needs. Ignorance or avoidance of these issues compounds any problems that exist. Silence on issues that matter is a form of rejection or complicity. It is possible for a worker to have made a referral for a specific service that will seek to meet needs arising from being disabled but to have never had a conversation about the experience of being disabled. In this situation, a disability is treated like a problem to be mitigated, almost as if it is separate to the individual service user.

Making complexity manageable

This chapter highlights the complexity of the task of working with people from BME groups. The field of mental health is complex in its own right. It demands a great deal of workers to take account of the uniqueness of each individual. Mental health workers have to overcome their own ignorance, prejudices and fears. This is clearly no straightforward task in relation to the mental health problems alone (Office of the Deputy Prime Minster 2004). Workers' own socialisation or lack of exposure to certain issues will mean that they are sometimes being required to act outside of their comfort zone. Even worse, they are asked to form empathic relationships when sometimes there is no empathy. An essential aspect of working effectively with BME groups is self-awareness. Cooper *et al.* (2006, p.24) state:

> The clinician–self relationship may be characterised as the degree to which an individual clinician is aware of his or her own background, attitudes, and values, and their impact upon behaviours and interactions with others in the context of health care.

Pursuing this level of awareness is not just the responsibility of white workers. Griffith (1977) outlines the need to understand and work effectively with various racial combinations of worker/client relationships.

This awareness will need to lead to continuous improvements in practice. When considering elements of a service user's identity a worker has to ask a range of questions, which are presented in Box 6.6.

BOX 6.6 EXPLORING PERSONAL ATTITUDES: KEY QUESTIONS

- How does this make me feel?
- How much do I know about how it makes the service user feel?
- What are the fears, prejudice and ignorance within myself that need to be addressed?
- What are the obstacles and discrimination in the life of the service user that need to be challenged, removed or reduced?

Training and peer pressure cause mental health workers to speak with conviction about ERC and to believe themselves to have an acceptable set of thoughts and feelings (Sainsbury Centre for Mental Health 2002a). The first question above, 'How does this make me feel', is not easily answered with absolute honesty. If this is turned into something specific it becomes clearer:

- How does it make me feel to hear a female service user saying that she would like support to go out and find a partner when I know she is talking about a woman?
- Would I feel differently depending on whether a service user of mixed heritage said that he identified himself as white or black? (If so, have you considered why?)
- How would it feel to have an African Caribbean man ask if it is OK for his male partner to sit in on an assessment to provide support and they sat holding hands and the partner was loving and supportive when the service user became distressed? Would it feel different than if his partner were female?

For many workers these questions may genuinely raise no feelings that they find hard to accept. It is likely that for some these questions will be less comfortable. Mental health workers are usually on a journey of development both personally or professionally. They may be drifting on a sea of change or rowing with vigour. The very least service users should be able to expect from front-line workers is a determination to offer the best possible support within their potential. There are seven elements that will strengthen practice when working with people from BME backgrounds who may have other identities as discussed in this chapter. See Sewell's Seven Elements for Strengthening Practice in Box 6.7.

BOX 6.7 SEWELL'S SEVEN ELEMENTS FOR STRENGTHENING PRACTICE

Be aware of possibilities

Own your feelings

Be curious

Ask empathically

Withstand and hold

Make sense together

Plan for progress

The consequences of the absence or presence of these seven elements are considered in Table 6.1.

Table 6.1 Sewell's Seven Elements of Strengthening Practice

Element 1: Be aware of possibilities

Weaker	Stronger
Lacking awareness of the possible impacts and experiences in relation to gender, being of mixed heritage, being LGBT, being from a BME group with white parental figures, being disabled.	Knowledge of how these aspects of people's lives could potentially affect their thoughts, feelings and behaviours and the experiences they encounter.
	Self-awareness and knowledge of the potential impact of these circumstances on the relationship between the individual worker and the BME service user.

Consequences

In the relationship with the service user the viewpoint of the world remains yours.	You are able to use information that is present in records or which emerges in the relationship with the service user as the trigger for exploring areas of identity and experiences.
Your conversations and assessments do not proactively consider matters that may have had, and continue to have a negative impact on service users' mental health and sense of safety (and actual safety) in mental health services and society. Your enabling and supportive skills operate at sub-optimal levels.	Any absence of information can be used to explore why aspects of the person's life that could be significant, are not salient in what has been said or written so far.
	You are able to make sense of an apparent incongruence between what is said and behaviour and this can be discussed with some understanding of possible reasons.
	Your work with service users does not perpetuate their experience of discrimination through a failure to consider their needs.

Element 2: Own your feelings

Weaker	Stronger
You repeat statements that are considered to be politically correct whilst having conflicting thoughts and feelings – but you do not work on resolving this.	You accept that the way you were brought up or the environment in which you live or lived will have had an effect on your views. Irrespective of your own relationship with the issues in this chapter you will be aware that you may have negative feelings and you will reflect on these either in a safe relation-ship or in a personal journal.
Your difficulties with some aspects of identity emerge in subtle ways such as passivity or slowness to act. The service user may notice that you remain silent about, or avoid certain topics.	You will reflect on what you consider to be the thoughts and feelings you wish to prevail and nurture these so that they are stronger in your internal conflicts.
At worst, you express displeasure about any of the matters discussed in this chapter. You feel that certain attitudes and behaviours pertaining to gender, sexuality or mixed relationships are wrong and because of a political, religious or faith conviction you feel legitimised in expressing these beliefs.	You will be clear about the possible ways in which your negative feelings and views may emerge. You will keep a mental check to see if you act in any way that accords with these.
The service users with whom you work may experience you as lacking credibility. At worst they find you discriminatory.	You will challenge yourself through reading and interacting with people who present arguments for alternative viewpoints.
	Your increased comfort and confidence will enable you to explore issues with service users. You will feel emboldened to tackle discrimination that they face.

Consequences

The service users may feel isolated from you in relation to certain aspects of their lives and this will strengthen their defences and weaken their engagement with you. Aspects of your work with them may be seen as good but will be limited. Opportunities for shared problem-solving and developing a care plan will not be optimised.	Your conversations with service users will help them feel confident that you have some appreciation of who they are. This trust will enable them to engage more effectively with you. This will open possibilities to explore painful areas in their lives, which when worked through, may help them on their journey of recovery.

Table 6.1 *cont.*

Element 3: Be curious

Weaker	Stronger
You are not interested in much beyond the presenting problems or 'symptoms'. Information that emerges about the aspects of identity discussed in this chapter is not explored unless the service user pushes this.	You are convinced, based on information from previous studies, that there could be a relationship between these identity issues and the service user's mental health problems or experience of services. You do not make assumptions but ask.

Practice

Weaker	Stronger
You do not return to the these matters if the service user does not immediately engage in discussion. You end up with a partial perspective on the problems faced by service users. They may interpret your lack of curiosity as lack of interest in things that are important to them.	You believe that the process of recovery involves service users finding their place in society. You believe that identity issues are important and that developing a positive identity is essential in psychological resilience. You try to explore and build on this with service users. You also know that people from BME backgrounds with the various minority identities discussed in this chapter experience discrimination as a result of their ethnicity, their mental health problems plus other aspects of their identity. Their experience of the world is likely to be hostile. You try to see if your role might help them tackle discrimination.

Consequences

Weaker	Stronger
They may, for good reasons, have become very defensive and would only discuss painful things if they were confident that you were really interested and worthy of their trust. Your preparedness to move on quickly from discussing these issues makes them default to closing down.	You make connections between service users' experiences and their mental health problems. The questions you ask convey your empathy and the fact that you feel that there is some sense to their distress, anger, frustration or disengagement. They feel more understood. This enables them to trust you more and the way they express their feelings changes. This strengthens their recovery process and reduces the extent to which their problems are expressed in ways that are destructive to them or others.

Element 4: Ask empathically

Weaker	Stronger
You ask little about the service user's identity. If you do ask, you do so in a way that is perfunctory. Your tone, eye contact and language communicates that you are not interested or that you do not feel comfortable asking about these issues.	You make no assumptions about service users' views or experience in relation to the various obvious or possible identities. You ask open questions without inbuilt assumptions, such as referring to a partner assuming a heterosexual relationship or assuming someone who is of mixed heritage sees him- or herself as black.

Practice

You state or indicate that you are required to ask about these matters. You feel obliged.	Your questioning and body language demonstrate that you recognise that there are potentially painful experiences associated with these aspects of identity. You listen actively and place value on the service user's views and perspectives.

Consequences

Your approach causes service users to close down on these issues. Service users keeps conversations limited to areas that they feel entitled to discuss such as symptoms, medication or social problems (e.g. housing).	Service users speak about their thoughts and feelings. They begin to make connections between aspects of their identity/experiences and their mental health problems. They make connections and draw conclusions about what might help in their journey of recovery. They honour you by including you in these processes.

Table 6.1 *cont.*

Element 5: Withstand and hold

Weaker	Stronger
If discussions about identity issues cause the service user distress you avoid the subject.	You listen carefully and try to maintain a safe environment for talking about difficult issues. You confirm that you expect the service user to be angry because he or she is likely to have experienced a lot of pain and discrimination. You provide boundaries to try to avoid anger being channelled into violence or inappropriate vitriol against you but you do not try to suppress it. You do not deny that you find it difficult or painful to witness distress or anger. You use this to reflect to the service user the emotions that discussing these things evoke.
If anger erupts, either towards you or less specifically directed, this triggers your own feelings of being attacked. You retaliate, perhaps unconsciously, such as pathologising the distress e.g. suggesting that the service user is ill or becoming ill.	

Practice

Weaker	Stronger
You amend the risk assessment to indicate that the service user is vulnerable to becoming unwell.	You find a place outside of your work with the service user to talk about any difficult feelings evoked for you so that you remain resilient.
Any reaction from the service user other than a positive engaging response is seen as an indicator that he or she is not resilient enough to deal with the issues.	You communicate your hopefulness that the service user will make progress in integrating his or her identity, whilst acknowledging the feelings and experiences he or she has at the time.
Suggestions by service users that aspects of their identity are not important in the work trigger your disdain.	If the service user seemingly rejects your attempts to explore issues of his or her identity you explain that the experience of many workers over the years is that there is a relationship between these issues and people's mental health, safety and recovery. Research indicates this to be the case.
You will be dismissive if they express disapproval or outrage that you are asking about sensitive issues.	You try to negotiate how questions are handled in future, if, for example, you as a worker feel that there are relationships between a contemporary problem and the identity issues that the service user does not wish to discuss.

Consequences

Weaker	Stronger
Any rejection or defensiveness that you demonstrate is perceived as a lack of empathy or at worst, a violation. You perpetuate previous experiences of rejection and discrimination. The service user's trust in you is undermined.	Your ability to withstand any intense emotions enables service users to be honest about how their experiences affect them and provides information that will be useful in making progress. This may be about developing their resilience of tackling discrimination they experience in their daily lives.

Element 6: Make sense together

Weaker	Stronger
You do not invest in trying to make connections between pieces of information from the service user's life.	You try to encourage service users to try to make connections between their feelings, experiences, triggers in their lives and their mental health. You work with their previous and current experiences of discrimination and traumatic experiences and consider this as relevant to their recovery.
Negative feelings and experiences are understood as triggers for an illness that the service user had a high propensity to developing.	

Practice

The effect on mental health of discrimination and internalised distress is downplayed; an attempt to remove or reduce symptoms is given primacy and is considered to be a connected but separate task from dealing with these issues.	You suggest that what the service user says or does (even if these are considered to be bizarre) communicates something. The detailed study of their personal history enables you to ask questions about specific incidents in their lives. You explore the detail around the times when their mental health became poorer try to work at understanding more about distressing life events that this may have connections with. You explain that the better the understanding of the connections, the better your ability to work through towards protective strategies.
The content of the work with service users centres on symptom reduction. Socio-economic problems in their lives are tackled only to contain or to prevent relapses.	
	Patterns begin to emerge in the service user's life and these help in anticipating difficult times and changing for the future.

Consequences

Deep-rooted issues that have an adverse effect on mental health are not tackled. Medication maintains a sense of stability but progress is limited. Even when service users' mental health is stable their lives are not fulfilling.	The process of recovery becomes more concrete over time, as plans can be put in place to try to break patterns.
	Self-esteem grows as service users come to terms with who they are and they feel more in control of their lives. They become more confident and their increased self-awareness means they are less at the mercy of the things that trigger deterioration in their mental and emotional state.

Table 6.1 *cont.*

Element 7: Plan for progress

Weaker	Stronger
The fact that you have become acclimatised to distress, disorientation and hopelessness affects your work. You have limited expectations of service users and do not persist in trying to find ways to help them make progress.	You feel honoured that you are able to be part of service users' progress in working through identity issues and perhaps being part of their battle for equality and fairness. You help set goals and remain optimistic when they feel desolate.
Service users' current stance on their sexuality, gender, mixed race identity or disability are accepted as permanent and you do not plan for progress.	You strengthen your sense of optimism by reading or hearing accounts of people who have succeeded in making progress. You seek out services that do good work on these issues and find out how they do it. You negotiate a way to help service users make contact with positive services that may be out of area, for example perhaps by spending longer on one contact visiting and shortening another or negotiating a longer space between sessions. You are creative in managing your limited capacity.

Practice

Your sense of invention has passed and your benchmark for success is supporting the maintenance of a service user's situation, rather than making progress.

Consequences

The service user becomes stuck and you do not have the motivation, creativity, knowledge or skills to help make progress.	Service users recognise that you see them as a whole person and engage with your optimism that things can be better.
	Together you make plans in small steps to tackle issues that may have felt off-limits to them and maybe previous workers also. You feel pleased to see the progress and your work becomes more rewarding.

The seven elements described in Table 6.1 require a commitment to the job that goes beyond just earning a salary. There are likely to be development needs for workers wishing to adopt these seven elements. It is important, however, that workers honour the fact that they are being afforded the opportunity to work with someone, delving into private and potentially fragile aspects of that person's life (Cooper *et al.* 2006).

Conclusion

People are complex and have many aspects to their identity, which have centrality at different times. The experiences of people from BME backgrounds who have mental health problems and who are from a sexual minority, of mixed heritage, women, disabled or who were brought up in public care face many challenges. Mental health services struggle to respond to the complexity of people's lives and front-line workers are sometimes out of their depth. Practitioners are encouraged to adopt principles that focus on the individuality of the service user whilst exploring issues based on the knowledge of patterns and trends.

CHAPTER 7

THE ROLE OF THE TEAM MANAGER

The management of teams includes responsibilities in relation to performance requirements of individuals and of the teams as a whole. The team manager must also ensure the development and support of excellent professional practice though someone else may deliver the function.

The distinction between business management of a team (and its individual members) and professional supervision is important. In social work teams it has long been the tradition for team managers to provide both functions (Bond and Holland 1998). Within statutory health services the clinical and managerial accountability lines have been different (Department of Health 1998).

Business and performance management of the team

The National Service Framework for Mental Health (NSF) (Department of Health 1999) sets out a standardised configuration of statutory mental health services in each area. Services are organised on the basis of teams with specific functions. These teams have managers who are responsible for a range of functions. The components of the role will vary but will inevitably include some management of resources (e.g. budgets, staff) and of performance (Scragg 2001).

The management of performance in relation to practice in mental health services is tracked through three primary routes:

- line management
- organisational performance management
- clinical governance.

All routes ultimately rely on the role of the team manager for improving outcomes for service users. An organisation's centralised performance management functions may identify weak-performing teams or individuals. Corporate performance reports may expose teams or individuals through the production of comparative information. It will, however, be the role of the managers at all tiers to set clear targets and processes for bringing about improvements (Waal 2007). Performance in relation to working with BME groups needs to be considered within this context. It is the responsibility of team mangers, whether in the community or in inpatient areas, to ensure that practice and outcomes meet agreed standards.

Clinical governance was introduced in the NHS in the document *A First Class Service: Quality in the New NHS* (Department of Health 1998). Clinical governance is defined as a framework through which NHS organisations are accountable for continuously improving the quality of their services and safeguarding high standards of care by creating an environment in which excellence in clinical care will flourish.

Four strands are identified:

- clear lines of accountability for the overall quality of clinical care

- a comprehensive programme of quality improvement activities

- clear policies aimed at managing clinical risk

- procedures for all professional groups to identify and remedy poor performance

(Department of Health 1998)

A team manager will need to give attention to the performance of staff who are accountable to him or her. The organisation's objectives should be clearly communicated from the team manager's own line manager and then to the team members. Fundamental to this must be the needs and demands of service users and potential service users. A team manager must know what is required and how to respond (Gilbert 2005). In addition to service users, managers will be responding to the needs of stakeholders such as general practitioners and other teams or individuals who may refer or take on referrals for service users from the team.

Business and performance management will cover a vast array of functions. With regard to managing service delivery in an ethnically diverse environment there are some key responsibilities of managers. These are well reflected in the three building blocks in Delivering Race Equality:

- better information
- community engagement
- more appropriate and responsive services.

(Department of Health 2005b)

Better information

If a team manager is to lead the provision of equitable services certain information must be known:

- the ethnic profile of the population being served by the team
- the distribution and clustering of particular groups
- the proportion of the team caseload from different ethnic groups, measured against the population as a baseline
- referral patterns by ethnicity
- critical data by ethnicity such as: admissions under section; repeat admissions; proportion of team's psychiatric intensive care unit (PICU) utilisation, by ethnic group; referrals to forensic services; referrals to psychological therapies and take-up; proportion of cases showing support with access to employment and education
- BME service user feedback, e.g. through the annual inpatient census, community mental health (patient) survey or the Healthcare Commission inpatient assessment
- Feedback from BME service users through local team feedback mechanisms (e.g. BME service user group)
- comparative data for similar teams in the organisation
- the organisation's overall data in relation to all of the above.

Though this seems a long list the information is, or should be, routinely available. The critical question a manager should ask is 'Is it possible for me to know whether I am offering a fair service if I do not know these things'.

Teams usually have sufficiently large caseloads for the manager to identify patterns of referrals, service utilisation and onward referral. Smaller units such as a crisis house or a specialist ward may need to rely on trend data over years. The team manager's role in relation to business and performance management will need to start from his or her own accountability for providing non-discriminatory services.

Interpreting data on ethnic variations may be beyond the competence of team mangers. The simplest starting point is to evaluate the service against these benchmarks. This will immediately begin to highlight areas for further scrutiny. See Table 7.1 for example if your team was a community mental health team you may look at the following:

Table 7.1 Evaluation of team performance

Disparities highlighted in research (see Chapter 2)	How our team perform
African Caribbean people have higher number of repeat admissions	Trust average for white group is 5%, for African Caribbean it is 12%. Our team performance is 3.5% and 15%
Indians people are under-represented in community mental health services.	The Trust has less than 1% representation of Indians. We have no Indian people on our caseload. Indian people comprise 4.8% of the local population

Having clear information will enable the prioritisation of corrective action (Kent 2004). Not everything will be achievable immediately but the process of prioritisation could include a range of criteria. These could include dealing with the greatest degree of variation first, tackling easy wins or making changes that require no additional funding. Whatever the criteria for prioritising the work programme it will be of benefit if the process is shared within the team. Examples of how data may be interpreted to inform work programmes are found in Table 2.1. The development of plans will be more effective if honest engagement is achieved with local groups so that they have a sense of involvement.

Community engagement

Community engagement needs to stem from a determination on the part of services and teams to make improvements. It takes boldness to draw attention to possible deficits in a service and an immediate consequence of engagement is a raised expectation that change will be forthcoming.

Team managers are left with two choices: either to avoid the issues or to expose themselves to scrutiny and increase their accountability to the communities that they serve. The most effective forms of change are those that include the input of the intended beneficiaries (Social Care Institute for Excellence 2007b).

When tackling performance improvement in relation to the provision of services to BME communities, team mangers should find ways to have honest dialogue with their local communities. This may be through a team-based neighbourhood group or through a service user group attached to a team or directorate.

Like all relationships the relationship between a team and the local communities will go through change. There will potentially be stages of intense anger or feelings of disengagement. It will be the manager's role to sustain the drive and commitment to involving others. Over time the relationship should move to being more collaborative. Communities may help in solving the problems that services have struggled with. They may be advocates for change or resources where team mangers have tried and failed within organisations. The brilliant practice guide produced by the Social Care Institute for Excellence (2007b) provides tools and well-researched knowledge for all managers, not only those in social care.

The approach taken to community engagement will vary depending on the local circumstances. A team-based general service user group may have themed events, focusing on ethnicity on one occasion, gender on the next. There could be subgroups and attention could be given to specific ethnic groups in different ways at different times. The priority needs to be twofold: to create a safe environment for people to be involved and to establish a mechanism that helps to improve services. It needs to be feasible within the capacity available and it must be sustainable over time. Key factors to take into account when consulting with people from BME backgrounds are:

- legacy of disappointments
- need for accessibility (location, language, times and dates)
- the perceived credibility of the staff present.

(Department of Health 1996)

More appropriate and responsive services

The team manager will need to use the links with communities and other mechanisms for feedback (such as service user surveys and activity data and research) to assess the degree to which the service meets needs of people from BME backgrounds. This may be in relation to the choice of intervention, volume, model or approach.

The concept of meeting cultural needs can be confusing as it may imply that people from minority groups have fundamentally different requirements. This is not the case. The outcomes being asked for by people from BME groups in all studies are consistent in suggesting that people would like food, shelter and safety; often they would like good relationships, something to do during the day, money, safe internal worlds and a context for talking about their problems (Bowl 2007a, 2007b; Parkman 1997; Wilson 1993).

There are many ways in which this responsiveness may need to be demonstrated. In one case it may be the provision of an interpreter to ensure that information is gathered accurately during an assessment or it may be referral to a therapist who is linguistically capable.

Team planning needs to build on the approach suggested in Table 7.1. This can be done using Table 7.2. Having considered the service utilisation data it will be important to gain an understanding of the views and wishes of BME groups that use the services.

Table 7.2 Template: Indentifying and responding to views of minority groups

What minority groups say	How we respond

Team managers are required to show leadership but this does not necessarily mean that they will have the answers to all the solutions needed. It is their role to draw out ideas from others (Gilbert 2005). In doing so the manager must safeguard against team members from BME backgrounds being held up as the experts, with responsibility for finding and implementing solutions (Dominelli 1992). This is not necessarily straightforward. Some people from BME groups may relish the opportunity to contribute some specialist knowledge (Brett, Behfar and Kern 2006). On the other hand they may be trying to compensate for deficits in the role of the manager. A team manager's role is to promote and engage in open discussion about the potential risks of BME members of the team feeling being 'dumped on' (Dominelli 1992).

Team managers are challenged with finding solutions where policy-makers and researchers have failed over the last 30 years and more (Department of Health 2003b). It is imperative that team mangers develop a systematic approach, where the outcomes being pursued are clear and where actions are developed and monitored in direct relation to these. In doing so team managers exhibit leadership rather than just being managers, the distinction being the ability to act on the basis of what is right and ethical as opposed to purely doing well as those things required by higher powers (Owen 2006).

Management of individual team members

It is the team manager's job to ensure that the people within his or her team maintain a focus on the people who are the end users (Social Care Institute for Excellence 2004). The workplace setting will have an impact on the ability of the team manager to have first-hand experience of the content of the work his or her team members undertake with service users. A ward manager may benefit from working alongside a nurse or activity worker whereas a manager of a community mental health team may be reliant upon case notes and other forms of feedback. It is possible that even in residential or inpatient services staff members may have significant periods of unobserved interactions with service users.

Often the absence of a negative comment is considered to be adequate reassurance that what is recorded or reported is a fair account of what happens. Trust serves an important function in the management of teams but part of the responsibility of a team manager is the requirement to have some assurance that the required standards are being achieved.

A prerequisite to providing a good appraisal of the work is having a clear sense of what good looks like and ways to turn this knowledge into reality (Kent 2004). Effective team managers will understand the difference between ethnicity, race and culture. They will understand the different responses that are required in relation to these.

Providing individual management on ERC is built on the same fundamental performance management skills as for any area. These are:

- providing clarity about expectations
- communicating these meaningfully
- ensuring that systematic reporting of actions by teams members are maintained
- utilising all sources of intelligence about the behaviour and performance of team members
- providing feedback about performance
- providing guidance about improving on weaknesses and resetting standards.

(Banfield and Kay 2008; Bond and Holland 1998; Scragg 2001; SCIE 2004)

These standard elements of good management practice often elude team managers as they grapple with the complexities of racism and discrimination. The emotive nature of the subject matter compromises the resolve of team managers. Criticism of a team member in relation to performance on ERC could be perceived as tantamount to an accusation of racism. A team manager who feels that his or her own practice record on ERC is not without faults may feel vulnerable about making this a central issue in discussions. It is these unspoken truths that often stand in the way of progress.

Provide clarity about expectations

Each public body is required under the Race Relations (Amendment) Act 2000 to develop a Race Equality Scheme (RES) that shows how it will promote equality of opportunity, eliminate unfair racial discrimination and promote good relations between all ethnic groups. It would be unjust to place the entirety of responsibility for delivering race equality on the shoulders of team managers. At an organisational level there is a duty to publish a RES and to ensure that the action plan is delivered.

A review was commissioned by Strategic Health Authorities (SHAs) in London in September 2005, three years after the first schemes were required by law. An organisation called The 1990 Trust had been commissioned to undertake the review of NHS Trust schemes, based on a trawl of websites. The review showed that all NHS Trusts had complied with the duty to produce a scheme, though not all were readily available on websites. The London SHA report showed significant weaknesses in the content of a number of schemes, when assessed against statutory criteria (The 1990 Trust 2005). The extent to which schemes had been implemented was measured through discussions and meetings with senior people in trusts who had responsibility for this area of work.

The statutory duty includes a requirement to publish schemes on websites. Failure to publish a comprehensively compliant scheme on the NHS Trust website was seen a fall at the first hurdle.

In November 2007 The 1990 Trust published the result of a review of all NHS Trust websites nationally for both 2006 and 2007. This showed that in 2006 60 per cent of NHS Trusts had published a scheme and this rose to 77 per cent in 2007. Compliance with aspects of the race equality duty was poor. For example, compliance with the requirement to publish the outcome of race equality impact assessments went from 7 per cent in 2006 to 16 per cent in 2007 (Commission for Healthcare Audit and Inspection 2007b).

The requirement that team managers are clear about expectations is not straightforward. In a press release, the Healthcare Commission expressed their concern about the credibility of widespread self-declarations of compliance with the race equality duty and announced their intention to inspect 40 NHS Trusts (Commission for Healthcare 2007b). A well-performing team manager is likely to experience dissonance if he or she works in an organisation where there is rhetoric about delivering race equality but where there is limited action at a corporate level.

It is within such a context that the leadership mettle of a team manager is tested. Effective delivery of race equality may require a manager to make a conscious decision to drive an agenda locally irrespective of the corporate systems (Gilbert 2005). This is not an unfair challenge. It is well acknowledged that corporate success requires leadership from the top but excellent organisations also benefit from having staff who embrace a leadership role at whichever level they function (Owen 2006; Peters and Waterman 1992; Waal 2007).

Once team managers are clear about their own commitment and role in promoting race equality they will be better able to identify expectations of their staff. In a well-managed organisation this will involve a stage where they explore with their own manager how they may apply local and national requirements at team level. An effective team plan will attempt to set realistic objectives and will pursue these relentlessly (Kent 2004). It is legitimate and often essential to work with the team on interpreting organisational requirements to apply these to practice (Leigh and Maynard 2002).

Even where models of best practice are available team members will still require clarity about what is expected of them, given time restraints, budget pressures, the particular service users with whom they are working and local circumstances. Team managers will feel different degrees of confidence and comfort with stating precisely what is expected but the greater the clarity, the more effective the manager can be in steering practice towards the best. Also, the greater the clarity of standards the easier they are to monitor.

BOX 7.1 EXAMPLES OF HOW MANAGERS CAN PROVIDE THEIR TEAM MEMBERS WITH CLARITY ABOUT PRACTICE

Team members should ask about a person's ethnic background as part of the assessment of his or her needs and not just to complete a box on the form. They should:

- ask about religion and language
- ask whether the service user requires an interpreter
- explore whether they have needs in relation to race, culture or ethnicity
- run a BME service user group to obtain feedback
- analyse complaints and critical incidents by ethnicity
- analyse referrals, service provision and onward referrals by ethnicity
- complete data returns to help compile a report that enables the senior management team/board to track performance on these areas
- ensure that discussions with service users include an exploration of how the service user's identity has led to experiences of racism and discrimination both within and outside services
- advocate in relation to experiences of racism and discrimination and do not deal with them as just part of therapeutic discussion
- ensure that discussions and explorations around ERC are part of the routine work and not restricted to the beginning of a new relationship with a service user
- ensure that the record of assessments and recovery-focused care plans in files reflect the depth of the work on ERC.

Communicating expectations of staff meaningfully

Like any section of the workforce, front-line managers will have different levels of knowledge, skills and commitment. Though organisations may have clear standards and monitor these, the translation of these standards to the front line may be weakened by the communication style of managers (Waal 2007). Only a proportion of communication is achieved through what is said. The Mehrabian and Ferris (1967) study that led to the widely referenced '7/38/55 rule' is often misinterpreted (Lapakko 1997). The assertion that 7 per cent of communication occurs through the words used and 38 per cent through tone and 55 per cent through body language is erroneous. The Mehrabian and Ferris (1967) study related to a very specific context of attitude communication and was a very small study. It is well acknowledged however that communication is achieved through a combination of body language, tone and words. Conflict between them is usually detected by an audience (Lapakko 1997).

Team managers influence the extent to which front-line workers carry out tasks with conviction. For example, the requirement to collect ethnic data can be presented as a meaningful part of finding out about variations in the provision of services. Alternatively, tone and body language (e.g. rolling of the eyes) when communicating the requirement to collect ethnic data can indicate that it is an imposed inconvenience. The impact of such discordant communication can be seen in the practice of front-line workers. Some either guess at the service user's ethnicity or they ask the question with the option to decline being presented almost as the preferred response (Department of Health 2005a).

Team managers do not bear sole responsibility for the problems that occur in communicating key messages. Organisations sometimes fail to communicate meaningfully through the management line. The issuing of instructions with insufficient engagement of managers weakens the chances of successful compliance (Kent 2004; Waal 2007). There are, however, some managers who are intent on obstructing progress across a range of matters; pursuing equity for people from BME is often a casualty of this approach. The many reasons for management obstruction will not be discussed fully here. It is worth noting, however, that amongst the more malevolent reasons, there is the possibility that managers either do not understand the rationale for a requirement or they feel that senior managers have failed them, for example with inadequate provision of resources. In discussing the challenge in healthcare management Walshe and Smith (2006, p.4) note, 'managers and leaders strive to balance competing, shifting and irreconcilable demands'. Other ways in which managers feel they have been failed include poor appreciation of operational implications of an instruction or poor choice of method to solve a problem (Owen 2006).

BOX 7.2 COMMUNICATING ORGANISATIONAL REQUIREMENTS: KEY QUESTIONS

Before communicating organisational requirements an effective team manager must consider some key questions:

- Is this the right thing to ask of my team?
- What end are we trying to achieve?
- Are there better ways to achieve this end? If so how has this been communicated to more senior management?
- What is the actual or potential impact on service users of not doing this?

Having conviction about a requirement may not remove all reservations but will certainly make the communication with the team more constructive. It will enable explanations that go beyond the unconsidered phrase 'I've been told we've got to do this'. Any act of a manager that undermines the possibility of achieving race equality contributes to institutional racism.

Ensuring that systematic reporting of actions by team members is maintained

It has taken many years for performance management to be applied to race equality. (Department of Health 2003c). This is yet to be fully embedded within current performance management regimes. Policy debates on this matter swing between seeking to place accountability for race equality on a par with other areas of performance and seeking to resist prescribing at a national level how things should be done locally (Commission for Healthcare Audit and Inspection 2007b). A consequence of this is that even where there is local commitment and the establishment of local performance indicators, delivery in relation to these is forever at risk from higher-profile priorities.

Team managers quickly detect which aspects of performance are likely to be most scrutinised. When juggling the resources available to them they will eventually focus more and more on aspects of delivery for which the organisation will hold them to account, i.e. the *real* organisational priorities (Waal 2007). Team managers who are committed to delivering race equality will need to establish a minimum level of information that they require to assure themselves that the practice in their team is acceptable.

BOX 7.3 ILLUSTRATION

Josephine, the manager of an early intervention team, established a set of information in relation to race equality, which includes targets agreed by the team and targets tracked through the organisation's performance management processes.
The NHS Trust corporately collected information on:

- the records where there is self-reported ethnic group data
- the proportion of cases where there was evidence that race, ethnic and cultural needs where taken into account.

Data sources were:

- the Trust's electronic service user records system
- team audits of a sample of cases.

Josephine asked herself 'How do I know whether practice and outcomes are acceptable and equitable for people from BME groups? If asked to produce evidence within 24 hours, what would I use?'

Josephine discussed these questions with her team and in relation to having an assurance that the team's practice and outcomes were acceptable and equitable she stated the following: 'If I am unable to tell someone how I know (rather than believe), I probably don't know.'

Together the team agreed that it was important that they knew whether there were variations in practice and outcomes in relation to people from BME backgrounds.

They looked at research and policy to determine the areas where variations were most likely.

They agreed that they would focus on the following indicators:

- readmission rates
- length of stay on wards
- engagement in meaningful daytime activity
- engagement in talking therapies.

They agreed their sources of data/information in relation to these focus areas, respectively:

- service user electronic record system
- service user paper file record system
- all members of the team agreed to keep a log for their individual caseloads
- all members of the team agreed to keep a log for their individual caseloads.

The team members developed a set of definitions of the indicators, with the help of others within the Trust. For example, they developed an agreed list of interventions that would meet the definition of 'talking therapy'.

Within three months of starting this piece of work Josephine was able to state with confidence that she knew that there were variations between the experience and outcomes for BME service users and those of white service users. She also noted that even before they agreed a set of plans to address these variations, changes already began to occur in the work of individual members.

The team reviewed the findings from their information and agreed that they needed to systematise the reporting of what they would do differently. They agreed a series of changes in the focus of their work. Team members agreed they would:

- explore further the impact of racial and ethnic identity
- explore the impact of racism and discrimination in the lives of the service users
- invest in building more trust in the relationships with BME service users by pacing the work differently so it had a less officious feel
- actively work on suggestions to the service user about taking up therapy and meaningful daytime activity but would do so with consideration and care.

The team discussed whether supervision was the most effective way of keeping track of the new focus in their individual practice. Team members made other suggestions, including developing audits within the team and the writing of reflective journals of work with all BME service users. The team agreed that any additional recording would create the risk that they would not keep up the process. They concluded that a combination of ideas would be most effective. They agreed that the practice would be picked up through monthly supervision. They also agreed that twice a year they would write a reflective report on their practice in relation to ethnicity and race. These reports would be used as part of preparatory work for the Care Programme Approach review meetings.

Utilising all sources of intelligence about the behaviour and performance of team members

Information about the practice and performance of each team member goes beyond the routine sources such as supervision or service user records. In the example in Box 7.3 the team explored data sources. Service users, referrers and other stakeholders provide a rich source of information. The challenges for the team manager include how they obtain the information, the relevance and value of the information and the reliability of the information. See Box 7.4 for sources of information.

Team managers could begin by carefully analysing a range of information. This process could be given priority during a two-week period. For example, a case summary produced for a court report or for any formal body may be silent on race and racism. A manager alert to these issues will ask

---

BOX 7.4 EXAMPLES OF SOURCES OF INFORMATION ON INDIVIDUAL AND TEAM PERFORMANCE IN RELATION TO ERC

- service user surveys
- serious incidents reports
- performance reports
- referrer surveys
- stakeholder surveys
- focus groups of all of the above
- complaints and compliments
- feedback through unstructured or informal comment.

---

some reflective questions about the practice of the worker, based on this. Typical questions might be:

> I noticed that despite the likely concerns arising from this service user's identity your report doesn't refer to any considerations in relation to his/her race or ethnicity. Please could you tell me what influenced you to omit this information?

> The report helpfully includes information on the referral to the BME day service but it doesn't say the purpose of this or what kinds of concerns were considered resulting in this. Are you able to demonstrate that you tackled discrimination and variations in experience and outcome in the work?

A manager who is keen to improve will always be on the search for cues about performance from various sources (Handy 1985; Peters and Waterman 1992).

Providing feedback about performance

This aspect of management has the ability to enhance or compromise an organisation's ability to deliver its goals. Telling a member of staff that what he or she did was not good enough causes discomfort. Good intentions to do so can be thwarted for many reasons. These include the wish to avoid the potential negative consequence such as the staff member's disengagement or just because the manager is not feeling strong enough for a confrontation (Banfield and Kay 2008; Kent 2004).

Racism and discrimination evoke such strong emotions that providing feedback on performance can cause team managers to feel even more discomfort than they might for other subjects (Williams 1997). The benefit of stating standards clearly in advance is that the conversation about failure to achieve standards can be neutralised. Challenges do not need to be charged with implied comment on the worker's values or beliefs in relation to ERC but remain as a routine performance management function.

Providing guidance about improving on weaknesses and resetting standards

The obligation for team managers to provide guidance requires that they know what good practice is and how to achieve it. The typical performance management cycle described in this chapter of setting standards; monitoring performance; providing feedback; restating standards; and enabling (e.g. through personal development or providing other resources) is the staple of line management (Banfield and Kay 2008; Kent 2004; Owen 2006).

With regard to working effectively with people from BME backgrounds the manager is required to be skilled and knowledgeable in providing advice on how to improve the practice so that the outcomes are improved. Team managers today are typically yesterday's front-line practitioners. Their advice on the detail of practice will come significantly from their own experience because they have had this positively reinforced through their promotion. There has been very little material published on what good front-line practice looks like (Fernando 2005). Some books offer vignettes as a means of illustrating learning points (e.g. Bhugra and Bhui 2001; Moodley and Palmer 2006). The transferability from one scenario to another is achieved through the critical analysis of the vignette. Good supervision requires an unpicking of the assumptions, motivations, skills and techniques underpinning positive examples (Scragg 2001).

BOX 7.5 ILLUSTRATION

Palvinder is a social worker. She is working with Ola, a 28-year-old Ghanaian man. Ola had recently been detained and had appealed against his section under the Mental Health Act. Palvinder had been working with Ola for nine months, visiting him at his home where he lived with his parents. His moods had become depressed after a period of three months, during which he had bought a lot of expensive clothes and items of jewellery. He had also bought some technical equipment to help him record his acoustic guitar music for which he was very passionate. Credit card and other agencies had begun writing letters demanding payment when Ola had been unable to meet his debts. His parents were concerned about the fact that their address would become registered negatively and this would affect their credit status. They were proud, well-to-do people and found this difficult. This led to significant tension with Ola and over time he became less and less communicative with them or anyone else. Palvinder had noted the deterioration in Ola's situation and had tried to work with him (and his parents on two occasions) to try to find a way to manage the debt. She hoped that this would help improve the relationship between Ola and his parents and consequently Ola's mood. One day she received a phone call from Ola's parents to say that he had stripped naked and had stood on the ledge outside the sash window at the front of the house threatening to jump. Palvinder arranged a Mental Health Act assessment and Ola was admitted under section. This was his second admission in ten months. Three days into his admission he appealed and Palvinder was required to write a social circumstances report. She maintained the need for continued detention as she believed that the stressful situation at home would still pose a risk.

Approach 1: Paula, Team Manger

Paula felt concerned that Ola's case had escalated and though Palvinder had been working with him the admission seemed to be accepted as an inevitable outcome. She felt that Palvinder should have been more proactive in providing advice and support on debt management. Paula also questioned whether Palvinder had developed a good enough relationship with Ola. She described to Palvinder a case held by Kirt, another member of the team. Kirt had worked well with a Ghanain young man who had been having difficulty with his parents. Kirt had managed to do some basic family work and had prevented the service user from being evicted by his parents, something that had been identified as a key risk to his mental health. Paula felt that Kirt had engaged well with the family's ethnic identity. He had spoken with them about their concern to not be seen as a failure by the system and through regular visits he had helped to calm the situation. He had also spoken with the service user about smoking cannabis and how his insistence on doing so at home was putting his relationship with his parents at risk. Paula explained that Kirt had spoken about ethnicity and had managed to engage well and advised Palvinder to try to apply the learning.

Approach 2: Jonte, Team Manager

Jonte expressed her concern that despite the team's target to reduce the repeat admissions for African and African Caribbean people she could not see evidence of any work to explore all avenues to prevent Ola's admission. Jonte reminded Palvinder that the plan was not to apply different thresholds at the point of assessment for an admission but to work proactively to reduce the likelihood that African and African Caribbean people would reach this stage.

She asked Palvinder how she had assessed the risk that Ola would be admitted. Jonte said that based on statistical evidence regarding African and African Caribbean people there was an increased risk to Ola that he be admitted. In particular Jonte asked Palvinder:

- What she assessed to be the contributory factors in relation to the risk?
- What had she assessed the protective factors as being?
- What was the evidence that she had mitigated the risk factors?
- What was the evidence that she had capitalised upon the protective factors?
- What theoretical frameworks underpinned her practice?

In relation to the first two questions Jonte asked Palvinder how she had taken account of the impact of stigma, racism and discrimination on Ola's experiences.

Jonte spoke about the work that Kirt had done and offered some critical analysis:

- Kirt worked with the family and took account of the different way in which their ethnic identity placed pressure on them.
- Kirt paid attention to the narrative when the family spoke and focused on why things were being said and how they were being said as well as the content.
- Counselling skills were used to strengthen the engagement.
- Kirt's work was underpinned by explanatory models. He provided space for the service user to explain his own

understanding of his experiences before and during his period of contact with mental health services.

Jonte helped Palvinder explore how she might have worked differently with Ola to achieve a better outcome. She suggested:

- After the admission nine months earlier, Palvinder could have spent more time discussing the factors that led to it and worked with Ola on a plan to anticipate and reduce risks in future.

- Palvinder could have spent time with Ola when he was overspending asking him more questions about his motivations. She could have used her knowledge that people who feel stigmatised or oppressed often seek status through material emblems of success to open up some discussion with Ola.

- Palvinder could have asked Ola about his understanding of his identity (incorporating all aspects of it) and asked him to explain how he felt this affected his life. She should have also explored with his parents how their ethnicity affected their level of tolerance for Ola's actions.

Jonte reflected to Palvinder that she presented a picture of seeing the likely outcome (i.e. Ola's situation leading to an admission) but being powerless to change them. Jonte asked Palvinder if this was how she felt and further, what might have helped her to feel more able to achieve better outcomes. They discussed shadowing another worker who is competent at working cross-culturally, reading material on working cross-culturally or involving someone with specialist skills or knowledge, even temporarily.

Discussion

The difference between the approaches adopted by Paula and Jonte relates to the attention given to the content of the work. Jonte demonstrated aspects of performance management by:

- giving feedback
- being able to explain what good looks like
- advising on techniques to improve current performance
- identifying resources or developments that might be enabling.

The role of the manager as an advocate

Team managers sometimes feel defeated in organisations where there are unrealistic expectations being placed upon them. This is often combined with pressure from the front-line staff to do more and their own personal conflicts about deviating from the reasons why they began working in mental health in the first place (Leigh and Maynard 2002; Owen 2006; Walshe and Smith 2006). People who fare worst in society and services experience a disproportionately poor impact from passivity. The manager who does not defend the need for prioritisation, resources and services for people from BME groups end up being complicit in a system that is poor at meeting the needs of these groups and does nothing proactively to correct this.

Good team managers will retain their commitment to advocating both for the service users directly and for their staff, as a means to improving outcomes (Social Care Institute for Excellence 2004; Tew 2005). Managers will need clarity about the targets for improving outcomes for people from BME groups and the standards of practice expected. In order to achieve these the team manager will need resources and support, such as:

- information about how services meet the needs of people from BME groups based on performance information and outcomes from complaints, serious incident investigations, service user surveys, etc.

- resources to support regular local feedback from people from BME groups about what they want from services

- language services to help overcome communication barriers

- agreement to prioritise the team's capacity for the groups with statistically poorer outcomes

- access to development for the team and for individual workers to use skills and knowledge in exploring the impact of race and racism in the lives of service users

- training that is tailored to the needs of the organisation and teams

- access to specialist BME services where these have been assessed as being able to achieve an outcome beyond the capability of the team

- advocacy services able to articulate the interests of people from BME groups.

Good tactical and communication skills will be required. The timing of requests and the mode of delivery will need to be targeted to achieve the best outcomes (Miller, Williams and Hayashi 2007).

Conclusion

It is clear that in relation to working with ERC the role of the team manager is demanding. Theories and models of management help managers to avoid being bewildered by every scenario as new. Providing services for people from BME groups is part of routine management practice. The challenge for a manager is to deal with these issues with a level of competence that is comparable with the areas of their best performance.

CHAPTER 8

THE ROLE OF THE TRAINING, EDUCATION, LEARNING AND DEVELOPMENT DEPARTMENT

The chapter relates to departments with responsibility for training, education, learning and development. It will cover the role of departments in informing the strategy of the organisation in relation to working effectively with people from BME backgrounds. The content of potential training, educational and development programmes will be discussed. It will cover the department's role as a commissioner and provider of training and development programmes.

Developing competence

There has been a shift in organisations nationally and internationally away from having a department with the sole functions of commissioning or providing training (Bloisi 2006). The focus on a 'training department' is becoming outdated as it emphasises training as a means of improving knowledge and skills over alternatives (Banfield and Kay 2008; Bloisi 2006; Owen 2006). 'Education, learning and development' conveys more accurately and more fully the mechanisms by which people move from current awareness, knowledge and skills to the desired level. Titles for departments include 'Learning and Development', 'Education and Learning', 'Education and Development'. This change in terminology is not purely symbolic but reflects an increased emphasis on the active role of the individual in learning (Reid and Barrington 1999).

Another flaw with the focus on training is that research highlights the limits of training courses in achieving sustainable change (Collin 2007). The possibilities for the design and delivery of training are numerous, ranging, from didactic courses to experiential/participatory models. Courses may be for a single half-day or run as modules over several weeks. Effectiveness in achieving the intended aims will vary according to the approach used. The costs will also vary and questions of cost-effectiveness and efficiency need to be considered also.

It may be naïve to assume that the intended aims of providing training are always to create a well-equipped workforce. The delivery of training sometimes enables an organisation to meet externally imposed performance requirements. For example, the national policy *Delivering Race Equality* (Department of Health 2005b) requires planners and providers of mental health services to receive training. Any assessment of an organisation's compliance with the policy requirement will measure the extent to which the workforce has received training. This type of performance management entrenches the model of providing training as the answer to development needs of staff.

Work has been undertaken nationally to produce a model for the content of training, the Race Equality and Cultural Capability training package (Department of Health 2007b). This is a laudable attempt to move away from a 'tick-box exercise' where the organisation is able to demonstrate that it has implemented a requirement with little regard for the standards or benefits. Relying on training courses still focuses, however, on the inputs rather than the outcomes. An organisation may demonstrate that a high percentage of its workforce has received training but it is less easy to demonstrate improvement in practice or, better still, improvement in outcomes for service users.

The creation of a standardised model of training is intended to increase the likelihood of positive outcomes. This implied causal relationship will become stronger as evidence develops. It will perhaps be possible to state in future that organisations that comprehensively implemented the Race Equality and Cultural Capability (RECC) Training package see measurable improvements in the key indicators of successful outcomes for people from BME groups.

The competencies required to work effectively with people from BME groups require the accumulation of knowledge, reflection on attitudes and the development or transfer of skills and techniques typically used within most of the helping professions. Not all of these are suited to the typical one-day training course that combines didactic presentations and workshop sessions. Whatever the content, training is most effective when learning is utilised in real-life situations as soon after the learning as possible (Collin 2007).

It is not legitimate to rely on the typical equation that suggests that if staff need their knowledge and skills to be improved this equals a need for training (Collin 2007). Some forms of development may best be achieved through reflection, either individually or as a team. It may be effective to learn through observing and critically analysing good practice by specialists (Bennett *et al.* 2007; Collin 2007; Kolb 1984).

The role of an education, learning and development department is broader than the commissioning and provision of training programmes.

Informing organisational strategy

Legislation, policy, performance assessment, local lobbying, service user feedback and organisational ethos all contribute to an organisation's wish to be more effective in meeting the needs of people from BME backgrounds. In organisations that deliver outcomes primarily through people the ability to achieve improved outcomes relies on identifying the most effective approaches and technologies and equipping staff to utilise them effectively (Torrington, Taylor and Hall 2007). Within this context technologies can be understood to mean theoretical models, approaches and systems designed to deliver specific outcomes (Fernando 1991).

In modern mental health services the drivers for improvements to services for BME groups are sometimes conflicting. Research outcomes indicate different things; various BME groups have different needs; and sometimes demands of local communities are expressed without regard for the operational reality. Leaders of organisations try to make sense of these various messages and equip their staff to respond appropriately alongside all the other demands being placed upon the system (Bennett *et al.* 2007). Departments with responsibility for education, learning and development have a key role in advising their organisations on how to interpret demands for training (Collin 2007).

Departments receive requests to provide training and these are sometimes unspecific or ill-defined. Examples of the kind of training that is requested are:

- equal opportunities
- diversity
- equalities and diversity
- cultural awareness

- cultural competence
- race awareness
- anti-racist
- anti-oppressive.

(Bennett et al. 2007; Ferns 2007)

Often those making the request use terms interchangeably and are perhaps not clear about what they hope to achieve. More effective education, learning and development departments explore the motivations that lay behind these requests. A problem arises if the organisation does not have access to the expertise to help managers to be more precise (Ferns 2007). A consequence of such a gap is that training may be commissioned or provided with very little consideration of the intended outcome.

Sometimes the organisational lead on race equality comes from relatively junior levels. Sometimes they have a particular outlook and approach that is reflective of personal experience and not linked to national requirements or an evidence base. Their advice may suffer from the limits of their knowledge, including suggestions regarding how development opportunities should be provided. It is common, however, that because of their role they are an assumed authority on the subject by top managers and directors. Education, learning and development managers have a role in challenging perceived wisdom.

Skills of negotiation, persuasion and selling may well be required if the managers of education, learning and development departments are to avoid being passive implementers of weak ideas or being locked in unproductive conflict.

Developing the knowledge and skills of the workforce: Getting from A to B

There are two primary concerns when considering getting from A to B, i.e. moving from the current position to improved knowledge and skills:

- What is the improvement that is required?
- What is the best method for achieving this?

Typically the first of these is defined by the organisational expert on ERC and the latter by the learning and development department, working with operational managers.

Managers of education, learning and development departments will help to unpick the required content by asking the questions in Box 8.1.

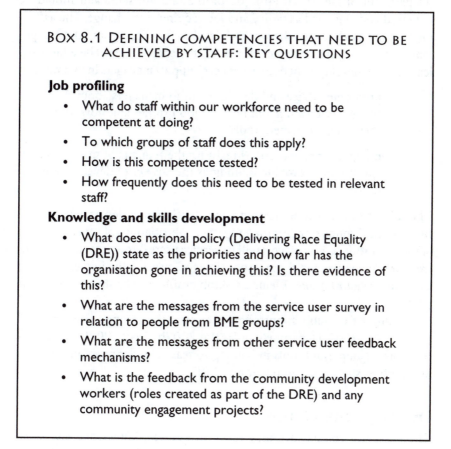

BOX 8.1 DEFINING COMPETENCIES THAT NEED TO BE ACHIEVED BY STAFF: KEY QUESTIONS

Job profiling

- What do staff within our workforce need to be competent at doing?
- To which groups of staff does this apply?
- How is this competence tested?
- How frequently does this need to be tested in relevant staff?

Knowledge and skills development

- What does national policy (Delivering Race Equality (DRE)) state as the priorities and how far has the organisation gone in achieving this? Is there evidence of this?
- What are the messages from the service user survey in relation to people from BME groups?
- What are the messages from other service user feedback mechanisms?
- What is the feedback from the community development workers (roles created as part of the DRE) and any community engagement projects?

In Box 8.1 the section on job profiling emphasises the connection between other human resources management functions and education, learning and development. The National Health Service pay and rewards system, Agenda for Change (Department of Health 2004b) sets out the model for designing jobs against a set of standards. Once the skills and competences of any role in the NHS have been set out the process of identifying development needs takes place between the manager and the employee. In NHS Trusts many jobs have a similar profile and the mechanisms to meet development needs are applicable to a range of staff.

Other organisations may have a less formal pay and development structure but will identify that certain staff within the workforce need to be competent in particular areas. The basic principle remains, i.e. that the more work invested in establishing a knowledge and skills profile for a role the easier it will be to determine the development needs of the post holder (Department of Health 2004b). Job profiles are not static and should be reviewed and amended as policy and job requirements change. The assessment of the gap between the worker's level of functioning and the competence required is the fundamental role of the team manger. The education, learning and development department can support managers in two ways:

- providing advice and development to managers about the process of creating and revising job profiles and how to use these as management tools

- on appropriate occasions resisting the requests of managers and executives to provide training as the answer to development needs.

The role of the education, learning and development department will be like a musical conductor, bringing together contributions of others to arrive at the end product. Key players will be service users through their feedback, front-line managers and those responsible for ensuring the implementation of *Delivering Race Equality*. Elements of job profiles can be shared for similar posts.

A number of publications attempt to state the competencies required (Bennet *et al.* 2007; Department of Health 2007b; Ferns 2007). These publications are important tools in helping to tease out clarity about job roles and profiles specifically in relation to ERC.

Defining competence

The necessary competence may relate to attitude, knowledge and skills (Waal 2007). These may also be in relation to specific aspects of ethnicity, race or culture (Bennett *et al.* 2007; Department of Health 2007b; Ferns 2007). The distinctions between these elements are not absolute but an understanding of the specific components will assist in the process of defining the competencies. Table 8.1 sets out an itemisation of the attitude, knowledge and skills in relation to each of the categories of ERC.

Thirty-five different competencies are listed in Table 8.1. It is improbable that all of these would be formally used to assess the competence of each member of staff alongside the various other areas that would need to be covered, from health and safety to core assessment skills. Organisations will need to identify a match between competencies and specific roles. It may also be necessary to have levels of competence (with examples of what this looks like in practice). A junior day service worker may need a different level of competence to an art therapist.

Table 8.1 ERC competencies

	Ethnicity	Race	Culture
Attitude	AE1 Shows appreciation of the value of different ethnicities AE2 Curious about how ethnicity affects service user	AR1 Engages with race as having a significant impact on experience AR2 Shows an appreciation of the social function of categorising people into racial groups	AC1 Shows respect for different cultures AC2 Identifies the elements of various cultures that are represented in society AC3 Shows appreciation that society is multicultural and that the prevailing culture has many influences
Knowledge	KE1 Knows key beliefs and behaviours of ethnic groups represented locally that might have an impact on the relationship between service user and worker/service KE2 Knows when to seek additional guidance on understanding potential influence of ethnicity KE3 Know where to access additional support	KR1 Knows how racism and discrimination affect people from the service user's group in mental health services and in other social contexts KR2 Knowledge of the social and psychological impacts of racism KR3 Understands how the social construction of race has primacy over biological aspects and how this operates in mental health services KR4 Knowledge of different types of active, passive or avoidance manifestations of racism and the appropriate response for each	KC1 Knows the difference between culture and race and ethnicity KC2 Understands the difference between experiences of racism, discrimination and being culturally isolated, overlooked or misunderstood KC3 Knows some key components traditionally associated with different groups and demonstrates an understanding of variations within the group KC4 Understands the difference between tradition and culture

		KR5 Knows the difference between institutional and personal racism	**KC5** Understands the impact of culture on the expression of mental health problems **KC6** Understands different cultural conceptualisations of mental health problems
Skill	**SE1** Includes assessment of the role of ethnicity in the life of the service user **SE2** Asks the service user about their ethnicity using his or her own knowledge of possible issues but without making assumptions **SE3** Uses additional support to overcome potential obstacles to ethnic needs being met such as gender difference, language or a sense of isolation **SE4** Constructs a recovery-focused care plan with service user taking account of the service user's ethnicity from his or her perspective **SE5** Integrates aspects of the service user's identity (woman, LGBT, disabled, mixed heritage) into the assessment and recovery-focused care plan	**SR1** Explores how racism and discrimination have affected the life of the service user **SR2** Uses the evidence of greater risks that people from BME will have poorer experiences and outcomes (see Chapter 2) to develop recovery-focused care plans that mitigate these risks **SR3** Identifies and tackles racism and discrimination in language, behaviours, policies and systems that affect the service user **SR4** Utilises appropriate support to enable the service user to develop positive relationships that allow him or her to tackle obstacles to recovery **SR5** Utilises personal and professional support to enable him- or herself as a worker to deal with the emotionally challenging aspects of dealing with race and racism	**SC1** Interviews to enable individuals to explain how they view themselves culturally **SC2** Asks the service user about his or her culture using the worker's own knowledge of possible issues but without making assumptions **SC3** Uses additional support to overcome potential obstacles to cultural needs being met such as gender difference, or a sense of isolation **SC4** Constructs a recovery-focused care plan with service user taking account of the service user's culture from his or her perspective

The education, learning and development department will be able to help managers in the organisation to separate out what may best be developed through different mechanisms such as shadowing, self-learning, supervision, mentoring, group reflection, etc. The need only arises, of course, where there is an individual or team gap between the competence required and how they currently perform.

Responding to gaps: The content of education, learning and development

Training programmes can be constructed from the content of Table 8.1. The race equality and cultural capability training programme (Department of Health 2007b) sets the design of training sessions in 12 modules. These are clearly set out and available to be downloaded from the internet and therefore will not be repeated here. The content of the training constitutes the latest policy guidance and reflects the most up-to-date understanding from research and studies into the needs of people from BME groups.

Other mechanisms for closing attitude, skills and knowledge gaps are:

- expert reflection, challenge and advice – consultancy

- observation of positive practice – shadowing and visits

- self-managed learning – reading and utilising online learning options

- team development – internal or external facilitation

- personal exploration and advice on skills – mentoring and coaching

- working with others doing similar on shared problem-solving and critical appraisal of learning outcomes – learning sets.

(Bloisi 2006; Collin 2007; Ferns 2007; Kolb 1984; Thorne and Mackey 2007)

These are applicable to ERC and the competencies shown in Table 8.1 as for any other areas of development.

Consultancy

In Chapter 4 (Box 4.3), an example is given of the work of Ade, a specialist who reflects back to a team member some analysis of his practice and offers advice. This is a useful model of skill and knowledge development because it is connected to a real-life situation, making it easier to apply the learning to practice. The education, learning and development department may have a role in helping team managers by providing a list of people or firms that may provide such a service. They may also offer advice about quality assurance for a consultant or specialist in ERC.

There are many people who offer their knowledge and skills around ethnicity, race and culture. Some do so without a formal qualification in the subject or any external validation of their experience and specific abilities. There are various qualifications that may be acquired, drawing on different schools of thought.

Some consultants may have some validation from satisfied customers but this may offer no assurance that they have offered something other than their own individual perspective, unsupported through current research findings or up-to-date national policy. It is a form of discrimination to apply lower standards in relation to the selection of a consultant to work in this field. Consultants in ethnicity, race and culture should be able to state the techniques they use in working with people (i.e. their basic consultancy skills) and also the theories and paradigms that they incorporate into the application of their specialist subject.

Shadowing and visits

It can be inspirational and educational to see practice at its best. The challenge in the field of ERC is that there is little benchmarking information against which to assess top performance. The national Delivering Race Equality programme hopes to be in a position to state that certain sites have implemented an approach and achieved improvements in the targeted outcomes.

BOX 8.2 ASSESSING EXAMPLES OF POSITIVE PRACTICE: KEY QUESTIONS

- How do you know you are successful (performance indicators)?
- Why do you use these as indicators of success?
- Describe your success against these performance indicators.
- What is the feedback from service users?
- What are the theories, approaches, models, techniques that are used to achieve the outcomes?
- Why do you use these as opposed to any others?

There should always be consistency between the intended improvements in outcome and the goals set out in *Delivering Race Equality* (Department of Health 2005b). There is widespread consensus that the content of this government guidance captures the key areas for improving services for people from BME backgrounds. There should always be evidence that local service user and community views have influenced the services and how they are provided.

Self-managed learning

There is a growing recognition that as people have different learning styles, self-managed learning or self-directed learning is growing as an approach (Collin 2007). The market is thin with relation to specific e-learning programmes as can be deduced from a quick search on the Internet. Education, learning and development departments have a role in identifying tools on the market. They may also take a lead or be involved in exploring options for developing or commissioning new material. This process may be carried out as part of a consortium to help share the set-up costs.

Other routes for self-managed learning include reading published materials. As with any development activity the learning should be designed in relation to an assessment of the gap between the required competence and current performance. The focus may be on learning about cultural or religious practices of a BME group that is represented locally in large numbers.

The use of learning logs or diaries is important where individuals carry out learning activities. Evidence may need to be recorded for demonstrating continuous professional development (e.g. for registration with a professional body). It may also be used for an organisation to demonstrate compliance with a performance management or contractual requirement to provide education, learning and development.

Team development

The development objectives of the team and individual team members should reflect the areas of weak performance against organisational objectives (Collin 2007; Scragg 2001). Sometimes learning can take place more effectively if the team has a common goal of improving in an area where they have a sense of shared ownership. This may arise because the particular outlook of the team embraces the area to be developed or because internal competition with other teams creates impetus. Whatever the motivation, it will be a valuable approach to focus on the outcome that the team is trying to achieve and to analyse the causes for the gap in performance. In Chapter 7, in Box 7.3 Josephine, the team manager, worked with the team to identify the components of practice that needed to be strengthened to achieve the desired outcomes. This work could have been undertaken with the help of an external consultant or facilitator. The process would be the same in that the whole team would work toward common development objectives.

Mentoring and coaching

Team managers are given the responsibility to lead their teams and many do not have the expertise in ERC. Further, they may have limited ability to deal with the emotions and challenges that are likely to emerge. Closing the gap on personal performance objectives requires admission of weaknesses and shortfalls. Some of these may feel personal and discussing them openly may feel very exposing. Working with ERC arouses strong emotions and fierce criticism at times. Admissions of failures are potentially interpreted as an admission of personal or institutional racism (Bhui 2002). Such an admission can evoke fear and hostility. A team manager may benefit from mentoring or coaching in such a context. Mentoring can provide guidance and reflection. Coaching provides guidance to perform a specific function or task (Gilbert 2005; Thorne and Mackey 2007). The education, learning and development department may have a list of people who are skilled in enabling managers to achieve specific outcomes, that are translated into improvements for service users.

Learning sets

Learning sets are typically groups of five to eight people who meet to reflect and learn together by bringing problems that they are all likely to face separately. Through structured analysis and solution-finding they plan for the future (Fry, Ketteridge and Marshall 2000). Learning sets are of particular benefit in relation to ERC as there is an absence of a body of evidence on what works to improve outcomes. Education, learning and development departments could usefully encourage the establishment of learning sets within the organisation and in partnership with others. Again, competent facilitators are key and the questions in Box 8.2 could usefully be applied here.

A learning set is most helpful if the people contributing are fulfilling a similar role and are working to achieve a specific outcome that is common between them (Fry et al. 2000). Rather than convening a learning set on improving outcomes for BME groups it would be beneficial to identify specific areas such as team mangers focusing on reducing readmissions or practitioners focusing on enabling African Caribbean people to access employment, education and training.

These are very specific and allow learning and obstacles to be considered. A learning set can choose to cover different topics over time but there should be a clear focus at any given time if they are to deliver to optimum levels (Dewar and Sharp 2006).

Getting from A to B: Applying the different approaches

Development towards the 35 competencies set out in Table 8.1 can be achieved in different ways. Table 8.2 (overleaf) presents a model that could be used between a manager and staff member to match the competencies to the development activities in a way that is bespoke to them and local circumstances. Under the 'development options' list activities such as reading recent publications, shadowing, recording reflections, discussions in professional supervision.

Conclusion

Training is often suggested as the solution to problems when performance is poor, service users complain or where other evidence of a skill or knowledge gap emerges. There is a range of mechanisms for closing the gaps. The use of a competency-based approach focuses more on the outcomes being pursued. Identifying how ERC development needs will be met should be undertaken with all the rigour expected of team managers supported by well-performing learning and development departments.

Table 8.2 Template: Matching development methods to competenciess

Competency	Development options
AE1	
AE2	
AR1	
AR2	
AC1	
AC2	
AC3	
KE1	
KE2	
KE3	
KR1	
KR2	
KR3	
KR4	
KR5	
KC1	
KC2	
KC3	
KC4	
KC5	
KC6	
SE1	
SE2	
SE3	
SE4	
SE5	
SR1	
SR2	
SR3	
SR4	
SR5	
SC1	
SC2	
SC3	
SC4	

CHAPTER 9

CONSIDERING ALTERNATIVES TO THE ILLNESS MODEL

Psychiatry is given prominence as a science on the basis that it was developed and continues to be developed on the basis of a large and robust evidence base and is consequently given primacy in analysing and responding to matters of the mind.

In the United Kingdom references to the illness model usually assume the approach of Western psychiatry. Psychiatry stems from the concept of pathology or illness (Fernando 1991). There are, however, non-Western conceptualisations of illness that do not rely on a medical understanding of Western psychiatry. Anthropologists identify idioms and words that indicate illness of the mind in many societies around the non-Western world (Fernando 1991; Littlewood, Jadhav and Ryder 2007). The responses in these countries and cultures indicate a difference in conceptualisation that is important to note. Fernando (1991) highlights the impact of Descartes, the French philosopher, on separation between mind and body, this division being clear and rigid in Western societies but less so elsewhere. The Cartesian separation of body and mind leads to practice that, at its most traditional, considers that illnesses of the mind require treatment of the brain (as a proxy for the mind) (Fernando 1991). Though this approach may not be strictly adhered to in modern psychiatry the Western psychiatric approach still views the impact of social factors as having an impact on the functioning of the brain. As such, treatment is provided to correct the malfunction of the brain alongside work resolving the social, emotional and psychological disruptions. The antithesis of this approach is a perspective that does not concur with seeing the mind/body division as concrete. There are significant pieces of work that present the evidence for seeing the inter-relatedness of mind and body (Levine 1997; Rothschild 2000).

The juxtaposition of Western psychiatry with other conceptualisations highlights the extent to which other cultures integrate mind, body and spirit (in terms of religion) (Fernando 1991). As Littlewood *et al.* (2007) point out, non-Western cultures are consistent in that they recognise evidence of mental health problems, which they describe variously, including the term 'illness'. They explain, however, that the subscription to a notion of illness does not necessarily generate a response that centres around a physical response, as is the case in Western psychiatry. This undermines the universal application of the concept of 'illness'. People in a society may be of the view that someone is ill but the response may be to pray for them (Fernando 1991). This crystallises a conflict of ideologies between workers and service users (Bhui and Bhugra 2002). This is problematic given that there is empirical evidence that outcomes are better when a service user feels that there is a shared perspective with his or her worker (Callan and Littlewood 1998).

The response to the defined problem provides insight into underlying assumptions. Further to the contrasting of the Western and non-Western beliefs about illness is the fundamental distinction between those who believe in mental illness and those who do not. One of the main criticisms of any model that is based on illness is that it locates a socio-political problem within an individual (Blackman 2007). Individuals are made to be scapegoats for the trauma and abuse perpetrated by others by determining that they are sick (Read *et al.* 2006). 'Alternatives to the illness model', when most narrowly defined relates to those based on the diametrically opposite end of the spectrum to Western psychiatry.

Irrespective of the confidence in Western psychiatry held by psychiatrists or staff in mental health services, there are people who do not subscribe to this model. Those who do not embrace the salience of the biological paradigm include psychiatrists and other staff working within the system. Many of these have published books and peer-reviewed research (Read *et al.* on the subject 2007; Romme and Escher 1993; Thomas and Bracken 2005).

Many people who would be considered as meeting the criteria for statutory mental health services have alternative paradigms for understanding their experiences. The Department of Health recognises this and in November 2007 launched a consultation on developing guidance for finding a shared vision for how people's mental health problems should be understood (Department of Health 2007d).

Psychiatry and race

The consideration of alternative models is particularly pertinent in a book on working with ERC. This is because of the history of psychiatry being used to justify racism or to view people from an overtly racist perspective. Fernando (1991) and Bhui (2002) outline various manifestations of this drawing on papers (including those subject to peer review) published in Europe and America between 1851 and 1978. The diagnostic label of drapetomania was used to describe the illness of running away. This was applied to slaves who tried to escape. Dysaethesia Aetheopis was a diagnosis of afflictions to mind and body applied only to slaves when freed. The use of language such as 'primitive cultures' was used in professionally reputable works in 1978. A new unclassified diagnostic label 'cannabis psychosis' emerged in the 1980s and was applied in the main to African Caribbean people. Culturally specific tools such as the Present State Examination are used cross-culturally. Concepts of emotional differentiation in industrially developed societies when applied to industrially developing countries and black Americans leads to judgemental view. Research has shown that race affects the diagnosis made by psychiatrists and the treatment and care given (Robinson 1995).

Leaving to one side the over-representation of certain BME groups in the psychiatric system, the link between race and mental health would still be strong. Both race and mental health diagnoses are classifications where the scientific benefit is small compared with their functions of social stratification. It is well accepted that the variations and similarities within and across races renders these categories ineffective as a basis for biological classification and study (Banton 1967; Rack 1982) (see Chapter 1). Medical diagnoses such as schizophrenia lead to a belief held in society that this is a specific and well-defined categorisation with reliable predictive value (TNS 2007). Schizophrenia describes a collection of conditions, and there is no physical observation of biological symptoms to support consistent, diagnosis or treatment. As one article in the *British Medical Journal* states: 'Schizophrenic disorders are a group of illness' and later 'There are no biological markers for schizophrenia' (McGrath and Emmerson 1999, p.1045). The diagnosis of schizophrenia does, however, enable both mental health specialists and society to draw inferences – usually very negative – about people (Read, Mosher and Bentall 2004; Whitacker 2004).

The apparent scientific basis for race combined with the apparent scientific basis for certain diagnoses such as schizophrenia leads to discourse that expresses social constructs as science (Banton 1967; Read *et al.* 2004). In reality social functions are being fulfilled rather than scientific ones. No biological or genetic deductions can be made based purely on the description of a person's race. No absolute conclusions can be drawn about medical symptoms purely on the basis of a diagnosis of schizophrenia. Research does, however, indicate that the greatest degree of predictability occurs in the combination of race and psychiatry. This is seen in the consistently poor mental health outcomes for people from the African Diaspora when trends are considered on any scale: across countries, counties and services (Singh *et al. 2007*).

This chapter explores alternatives to the illness model against the backdrop of concerns about the experiences, and not just the outcomes, of people from BME backgrounds in mental health services (Commission for Healthcare Audit and Inspection 2007a, 2007b; Mental Health Act Commission 2006). Whether because of tradition or a wish to avoid the impact of psychiatry, people utilise alternative models to understand and respond to their experiences. McCabe and Priebe (2004), in their study of the differences in explanatory models across ethnic groups, identified that people from BME backgrounds are significantly less likely to utilise the biomedical model, and are more likely to use supernatural or social explanations for their experiences.

Faith and religion

Faith and religion are often linked but have distinctive features. Faith is a belief in a deity or deities: a being or beings with power greater than human. This may be expressed alone or in a group and provides a belief system that guides daily living (Department of Health 2003d). Religion is described as the organisation of faith and other beliefs. Religion has a recognisable belief system, traditions, rules of engagement and community (Hilton, Ghaznavi and Zuberi 2002). It creates structure, order, regularity and routine. Faith may be expressed within a community or faith group but the emphasis is on the beliefs and adhering to these as opposed to the rules that govern membership.

Spirituality is simply the essence of being, which recognises that experiences transcend those defined only by five senses that relate to the physical world (Department of Health 2003d). It may encapsulate faith and religion but is defined more loosely because it does not emphasise belief in a deity, codes or rules. It relates to experiences that are personal. Faith and religion may be the expression of someone's spirituality.

There is an increasing recognition that people cannot be defined only by their physical, mental, psychological and social characteristics (Coyte, Gilbert and Nicholls 2007). Belief systems provide constructs for making sense of the world and these apply in mental health as anywhere else (Feifel 1958). Government policy-makers in England have been placing greater emphasis on the need for mental health services to take account of the spiritual needs of people. Their spirituality may provide some protective and healing value in relation to mental distress. This was identified as a theme in a study of the experience of women from BME groups in mental health services (Chantler 2002). Religiosity has been cited in studies as providing a protective element in relation to suicide (McKenzie, Serfaty and Crawford 2003). The positive role of spirituality, including faith and religion, in recovery is well documented in Coyte *et al.* (2007). One implication of the centrality of religion or faith is that the expressions of distress or disorganised thought might utilise the associated language and concepts.

Fernando (1991) conducts a useful review of religions in African, Eastern and Native American societies. They manage an integration of religion with other aspects of human experience thus avoiding the Western dichotomy between mind and body. As Feifel (1958, p.565) states, 'In Hinduism, for instance, psychology and religion are the same subject and always have been so.'

The purpose of including faith, religion and spirituality in this chapter is not to provide detailed insights into the various forms across the world. The purpose is to understand how these might feature in the way in which mental health problems are considered, understood and expressed by people from BME backgrounds who are living with mental health problems.

When considering religion, faith and spirituality four main aspects emerge about how they serve as alternative models to Western psychiatry:

- as explanations for experiences
- as aspects of identity
- as protective factors
- as mediums through which mental health problems are manifested.

Practitioners in mental health services may have personal views and commitments with regard to a religion or faith. It is the function served in relation to the service user that must define what is given prominence in the therapeutic relationship. There are both common and obscure religious, faith or spiritual concepts and idioms. It would be unrealistic to expect each worker to be an expert in all religions and faiths of the world. It is reasonable to expect workers to have some interest in, and knowledge of the main religions and faiths of all groups significantly represented in the local area.

For some BME groups their ethnic identity and their religion or faith is inextricably linked. Failure to take account of spirituality, faith or religion may lead to a perception of racist practice. As faith and religion is more central to many BME groups a blanket failure by an individual or service to consider these does have a disproportionate impact. As with many subjects that might emerge from service users, a safeguard against misunderstanding is the building of trusting therapeutic relationships.

Hearing Voices Approach

The Hearing Voices Approach represents the antithesis of Western psychiatry in its opposition to the attempt to fragment humans conceptually into minds and bodies and in the location of illness in an individual. The National Hearing Voices Network (HVN England) is part of an international network, Intervoice. The network supports the understanding of experiences of hearing voices, seeing visions and having unusual perception as carriers of important messages. Understanding is gained through engaging with these experiences, listening to voices and being supported to understand their meanings. Recovery is achieved by working through the consequences of what have usually been traumatic experiences in life and this requires attention to be given to often very painful things. The voices serve as a form of internal communication of the need to address these.

The philosophy of the Hearing Voices Approach is self-help. This is supported through a network of Hearing Voices Groups. The aim is for all Hearing Voices Groups to be facilitated by people who hear voices. Hearing Voices Groups that operate according to the approach work to key principles:

- Voices are meaningful and are engaged with as carriers of messages that are important to the individual.

- People are supported to live with their voices and not to eradicate them.

- Discussing experiences in a safe environment allows for the mutual sharing of techniques for people to keep themselves safe and make sense of their experiences.

- Facilitators are trained and accredited to ensure they have the necessary competence to run a group.

- Facilitators will be people who hear voices (voice hearers) but where a group is embryonic, for a transitional period of around six months, a professional may co-facilitate.

The National Hearing Voices Network (UK) has a clear statement of philosophy and guiding principles that all affiliated groups agree to adhere to. This enables the network to safeguard the approach so that is does not become bastardised through the development of groups that deviate from the key principles.

There is a growing evidence base, with many accounts of people who have regained control over their lives through the Hearing Voices Approach. A forthcoming anthology entitled *Recovered Voices* by Professor Marius Romme, Dr Sandra Escher and Jacqui Dillon presents voice hearers' accounts of recovery outside of traditional biological psychiatry whilst continuing to hear voices.

There are more than 160 Hearing Voices Groups in England affiliated to HVN. There are groups operating in more than 20 countries, covering all continents.

The Hearing Voices Approach has resonance for people from BME backgrounds because its philosophy is the antithesis of the biological and medical model. The traditions of many non-Western societies are not based on the Cartesian separation of body and mind (or soul) (Fernando 1991). One of the most consistent themes across studies that look into the experience of people from BME backgrounds in mental health services in the UK is the wish to avoid the degree of reliance on medication as found in psychiatry (Parkman *et al.* 1997; Wilson 1993). BME service users often report a search for additional or alternative ways to manage their mental health problems. Exploring these possibilities is one of the functions of Hearing Voices Groups.

Front-line workers may encounter service users from BME groups who speak about their experience in a way that concurs with the Hearing Voices Approach. There may be a group within their organisation locally and their employing organisation may have a view on the Hearing Voices Approach that either supports or prohibits involvement. The organisation may be agnostic and the worker will make a decision about involvement based on his or her own judgement. Workers may however find that the organisational culture limits their role in referring or advising a service user about involvement in a Hearing Voices Group or utilising the approach. They may find their role is to listen, understand and to use their skills to work with the service user effectively, taking account of their perspectives.

Trauma approaches

Studies have shown that most laypeople make an association between trauma and mental health problems (Read *et al.* 2006). Mental health policies routinely acknowledge the relationship between trauma, stress and mental health problems (Department of Health 2004a, 2005b).

There is a common-sense approach and also a reliable evidence base for the relationship between trauma and mental health problems. Read *et al.* 2005 present a body of evidence supporting the view that the relationship is causal. This is distinct from the stress vulnerability model, which identifies the relationship but sees the trauma as a precipitating factor where there is a pre-existing propensity towards developing an illness, as critiqued by Blackman (2001).

People from BME backgrounds routinely report racism as a cause or causal factor in their mental health problems (Bowl 2007b). Studies in different countries have referred to the toxicity of the environment as a probable cause of the raised level of mental health service use by African Caribbean people (Veling *et al.* 2007). Singh *et al.* (2007) argues that toxicity of the environment does not explain the degree of variation specifically in relation to people from African and African Caribbean backgrounds. This does not take account of either Toxic Interactions Theory (see Chapter 2) or the intergenerational trauma arising from slavery (Crawford *et al.* 2003; Davis 2007; Fanon 1967; Montgomery 2005).

Mental health workers seeking to take account of the trauma model when working with people from BME backgrounds (and specifically people from African and African Caribbean groups) will need to consider five components:

- the causal relationship between trauma and mental health problems

- that racism, discrimination and slavery constitute trauma

- the intergenerational impact and manifestation of trauma

- that there is intergenerational trauma in the African Diaspora as a consequence of slavery

- that there may be other compounding traumas such as sexual or physical abuse.

The causal relationship between trauma and mental health problems

Read *et al.* (2006) set out the quantitative and qualitative research evidence for the causal link between trauma and mental health problems. There are three main obstacles present for those finding it difficult to accepting that the link is direct and causal. These are:

- internal ideological conflict

- the salience of research that promotes a purely biological approach or stress-vulnerability approach

- the separation in time between events and the manifestation of mental health problems, or the fact that a series of small events have a cumulative impact that is traumatic.

Internal ideological conflict is seen in the idiom 'there but for the grace of God go I'. This phrase makes the statement that it is not the individual who carries a propensity but that the reactions are 'normal' given the abnormality of the circumstances. This is the fundamental argument of supporters of the trauma model (Blackman 2007; Bloom 1997; Read *et al.* 2006; Romme and Escher 1993). The ideological conflict is displayed in the practices of those in mental health services who understand the impact of trauma but also utilise a biological explanation for mental health problems. This is compounded by the variability in the way that trauma is understood.

The salience of research that promotes a purely biological approach or stress-vulnerability approach establishes this as the foundation of mental health services. Many workers in mental health believe that it is irrefutable that there is a biological cause based on studies of brain chemistry involving families and mono-zygote twins separated at birth. However, the research studies informing this position have been reviewed and their weaknesses demonstrated by Joseph (2003). Thomas and Bracken (2005) have undertaken a deconstruction of the research underpinning the biological model. Theirs is part of a large body of writing on alternative perspectives but this is not as prominent or plentiful as material on the biological model. Workers operate in a social and political environment that promotes and utilises the biological model.

The statistics that 64 per cent of women who use inpatient mental health services have suffered from physical and/or sexual abuse (50 per cent child sexual abuse specifically) make the arguments for the relationship between abuse and mental illness (Read 1997). Direct (causal) links between events and mental health problems are harder to make because the reluctance to disclose, the time delay between incidents and them being reported, and diffuseness of the trauma allow the introduction of other variables considered to have an influence (Spauwen *et al.* 2006). Other variables include biological changes such as dopaminergic abnormalities, one of the key foundations of the biological model of mental illness (Read *et al.* 2001). Reluctance to discuss traumatic events may be protective because of embarrassment, shame or concern about triggering an adverse emotional or psychological reaction (Hardy *et al.* 2005; Spauwen *et al.* 2006)

Racism, discrimination and slavery as trauma

Racism, discrimination and the consequences of slavery are not salient in care plans, and the government's policy *Delivering Race Equality* argues the need for change in this area (Department of Health 2005b). Slavery was a traumatic episode. Descriptions of both individual lives and societies as a whole demonstrate this clearly (Fanon 1967; Wright 2006).

The intergenerational impact and manifestation of trauma

There is an increasing recognition of the intergenerational impacts of slavery (Crawford *et al.* 2003). There are various terms applied to this disturbing phenomenon, such as post traumatic slave syndrome (Crawford *et al.* 2003). This transmission of trauma-reactions to subsequent generations is researched also in relation to the offspring of holocaust victims (Wiseman *et al.* 2006) and Aboriginals (Quinn 2007). Offspring display behaviours that experienced professionals would readily identify as those exhibited by someone who had been abused or exposed to trauma.

Working with the concept of intergenerational trauma in modern mental health services

As knowledge of this concept becomes more widespread in black communities it will be used as an explanatory model more frequently. Workers may have their own views about the relevance of the trauma model or the intergenerational impact of slavery. Some may actively explore these perspectives further in an attempt to broaden the perspectives underpinning their practice. Workers may find that whatever their own view, service users will speak about their experiences using the paradigm set out here. An approach that disregards the perspectives of service users whilst trying to promote a positive relationship will be weak in achieving engagement (Bhugra 2002).

The views of service users and their families may well be expressed in similar terms to Crawford *et al.* (2003, p.269):

> It is not plausible that after two centuries of relentless oppression and brutal violence, slavery simply ended leaving no trace of its psychological impact upon the generations that followed. The evidence of the transmission of the psychological effects is represented in racial economic disparities, consumerism, higher rates of morbidity and mortality for many diseases and decreasing overall life expectancy.

There may be other compounding traumas such as sexual or physical abuse

ERC may be salient features that trigger experiences that lead to mental health problems. Usually there is a complex mix of issues that affect people's mental health and it will be important for workers to avoid narrowing their analysis to factors associated with ERC. For example, the trauma arising from child sexual abuse cited by Read *et al.* (2006) is no less applicable to people from BME groups. The consequences of multiple stressors and traumas can have a compounding negative effect on mental health.

Recovery Approach

Recovery can be defined as:

An individual journey defined by the individual, driven by hope, and which focuses on achieving personal control and purposefulness rather than the eradication of symptoms. Recovery is therefore not seen as an absolute outcome in relation to an illness but a process of pursuing aspirations and reclaiming a fulfilling role and position in society.

(Based on Department of Health 2004a, 2005c;
Social Care Institute for Excellence 2007a)

Front-line workers will find a conflict of ideologies and approaches if they operate within a Western psychiatric model and the service user pursues the Recovery Approach. The Recovery Approach is not necessarily anti-psychiatry (Social Care Institute for Excellence 2007a). People utilising the Recovery Approach may, however, adopt an oppositional view to psychiatry. Mental health services are driven by risk management and this often has the consequence of limiting creativity and optimism (see Chapter 4). The Recovery Approach embraces risk assessment and risk management but also promotes positive risk-taking. Positive risk-taking is, however, only possible if based on effective risk assessment and management. Supporting someone who still feels fragile back into employment will require an assessment of the risks and development of a plan to ameliorate these. Service users describe mental health services as eroding hope rather than promoting it (Office of the Deputy Prime Minister 2004). There are also many causes for loss of hopefulness in workers, including the fact that they become jaded by their experience of repeat admissions and reinforced perception of little progress in the lives of service users (DeSisto *et al.* 1995). People from BME backgrounds experience the impact of this lack of hopefulness because of:

- poorer engagement and communication and therefore poorer empathy

- negative stereotypes about the limited capacity of BME groups to achieve mental or social recovery.

Working with the Recovery Approach requires workers to embrace the hopefulness of service users and on occasions be the ones promoting this. The Recovery Approach requires that each individual is given the right to expect positive risk-taking. The bespoke approach of service users to find their way through life, including their mental health problems, is respected within the Recovery Approach. Strong practice is seen when workers explore the approaches and ideas of the service user and recognise the capacity this approach has for arriving at solutions. These solutions may overcome small obstacles on their journey towards their goals.

Explanatory models

Explanatory models enable service users to describe their experiences, whether they define them as an illness or not, according to their under-standing of cause, reason for persistence and strategies for treating, coping or recovering (Bhui and Bhugra 2002, 2004; Littlewood *et al.* 2007; McCabe and Priebe 2004).

Cultural Formulations are specific approaches based on using explana-tory models. They provide prompts (but not structured questioning) to explore the place of culture and its interaction with other components of explanations offered by service users (Bhui and Bhugra 2004). Kleinman and Benson (2006) provide an accessible guide to cultural formulation. They suggest a series of steps in questioning, covering ethnicity, cultural influences and narratives about service users' experiences and what is at stake.

The concept of Explanatory Models is rooted in psychiatry. The accep-tance of alternative models is seen as the service user's perspective and language for what is a psychiatric illness. Embracing Explanatory Models is perhaps the limit of those working within mental health services, certainly in terms of what they would articulate and maintain credibility in their roles.

Alternative models and the impact on practice

There are a number of techniques and approaches available to front-line workers to enable the alternative models held by service users to be incorpo-rated into their work. These are primarily approaches to utilise service users' explanatory models in assessment and planning. Bhui and Bhugra (2002) highlight the challenges to the use of explanatory models in psychiatry and mental health services more widely. These include the conflict with the bio-medical basis of psychiatry and the limits of workers' skills in utilising the skills rooted in social sciences.

Conclusion

Practitioners in mental health services operate in an environment where alternative models are not regarded as having the same scientific credibility as psychiatry. People from BME backgrounds are more likely to seek expla-nations for their experiences in models other than psychiatry. Knowledge of various perspectives will enhance the work of practitioners, as will a better appreciation of the relative strength of the research underpinning psychiatry and its alternatives.

CHAPTER 10

POSITIVE EXAMPLES OF DOING IT DIFFERENTLY

One of the most pressing needs in relation to working with people from BME backgrounds is establishing a body of evidence on what works.

The basic human needs of people from BME groups are the same as for white people. This acknowledgement is central in the approach to considering positive practice. The provision of culturally tailored psychological intervention is not primarily about meeting cultural needs but about enabling the human needs to be met in relation to the relief of distress. Ethnic, racial or cultural specific interventions or approaches merely remove the barriers to people being able to derive benefit. It is this orientation that is crucial, i.e. focusing on the potential for service user benefit.

When reduced to their fundamentals, the treatments, technologies and approaches used to help with mental health problems most effectively are the same irrespective of the background of the service user. There are no magic solutions. There are no ethnic, cultural or racial interventions that do not rely on the basic building blocks of modern mental health care. This fact is liberating. It is clearly not beyond the capability of all mental health workers to augment their knowledge and skills so that their practice is effective with people from BME groups. There may be occasions when the specialist knowledge or abilities are required, such as those of an interpreter may be needed or a same-language therapist. Sometimes better engagement is enabled through the involvement of a specialist worker from the same or similar ethnic background. Even this involvement of specialists is within the core skills of mental health workers. The skill is to appreciate the urgency of needs and recognise when the worker has reached the limits of his or her knowledge and competence. For example, specialist benefits advice might be sought where this is important in the recovery-focused care plan. Workers recognise the need and the risk of not getting it right.

In the application of skills and knowledge in mental health services there are key areas where an emphasis is different or where there are different conceptualisations for people from minority ethnic groups. For example, there are cultural and ethnic specific approaches to psychotherapy (Kareem and Littlewood 1992). Miranda *et al.* (2005) write about the cultural adaptations to cognitive behavioural therapy in their comprehensive review of psychosocial interventions for people from minority ethnic backgrounds. There are ethnic and cultural specific day services and residential services. There was even an African Caribbean inpatient service in Birmingham, called the Pattigift Centre which closed in 2007 due to insufficient numbers of referrals. The Ipamo service described in Fernando (2005) developed a model to integrate outreach, community engagement and crisis care in a residential context. The philosophy of the service was to keep black racial identity central and to utilise traditional African and African Caribbean conceptualisations of life challenges (not just of mental health problems). These examples all demonstrate that providing safe environments and developing positive and therapeutic relationships underpin alternatives to mainstream services. This is not intended to down play the need for alternative or amended dimensions.

There are two primary questions when thinking about such examples:

- Do they provide a service that is better and more effective?

- What is the essence of the difference and could this be transferred to other providers?

These primary questions include concepts and terms that require further exploration. Waal (2007) explains the need for clarity about the critical success factors (CSFs) for an organisation, which are measured by key performance indicators (KPIs). He goes on to describe the link between the high corporate strategic CSFs and those for the organisation's service delivery units. Key processes required to achieve the CSFs need to be understood and monitored so that KPIs can be achieved.

The phrase 'better and more effective' is considered in detail in many clinical (or professional) and management articles. 'Better' will mean different things depending on who is defining this. Service users may consider the provision of counselling and social support to be better than inpatient provision. Services charged with protecting the public or reducing the risk of harm to service users as their core objective will prioritise services and outcomes centred on these aspects.

An organisation's definition of a successful internal service delivery unit may unearth a conflict in the organisation about CSF or key processes.

Examples of positive practice may be well regarded by service users or organisations nationally and internationally but may represent teams with CSFs that are divergent from those of their organisations'.

Positive practice as a concept is therefore more complex than might first be apparent. There is a need to understand the difference between inputs, outputs and outcomes (Waal 2007). The outcomes may be described in relation to the organisational outcomes or the end user outcomes.

BOX 10.1 DEFINITIONS

Critical success factors
Critical success factors in mental health services include ensuring the health and safety of service users and others.

Inputs
Critical success factors that are processes and efforts and are considered to be pre-determinants of the desired outcome. For example, 'seven-day follow-up' is a process factor in reducing the number of people who commit suicide after discharge from psychiatric hospital.

Outputs (organisational outcomes)
Achievement of factors that demonstrate that the organisation is delivering changes to trends and patterns. These are usually represented as key performance indicators. For example, a reduction in the numbers of suicides in the 7 days following discharge.

Outcomes (end users)
Improvements in the mental health and circumstances of service users (i.e. their recovery) so that they no longer need mental health services that have protection of health and safety of the service users and others as the first amongst their critical success factors.

Exploring examples of positive practice

This section looks at three services that are considered to be examples of positive practice and poses a series of questions to deconstruct the two primary questions stated earlier. The set of questions are listed in Box 10.2.

The search to find evidence of positive practice is confused by an approach that operates as if there is one problem that will lead to a single

---

BOX 10.2 QUESTIONS FOR ASSESSING EXAMPLES OF POSITIVE PRACTICE

- What outcomes are being pursued?
- What outcome measures are used?
- Why have these measures been chosen?
- What methods are used to try achieve these?
- Why were these methods chosen?
- What is the description of the direct work with service users in relation to:
  ° racial and ethnic identity
  ° racism and discrimination
  ° race/ethnicity in relation to other aspects of identity
  ° a focus on recovery?
- What are the key indicators used by the organisation to evaluate its success?

---

solution achieved through a single identifiable input. Positive practice is best considered as one way of overcoming a specific problem or set of problems. There are likely to be themes across examples of positive practice and for those considered in this chapter it is the quality of relationships, as considered in Chapter 5.

Mellow Campaign, East London NHS Foundation Trust

AIMS

Mellow describes its aims as to reduce the over-representation of young African and Caribbean men in mental health services and to develop alternative responses to mental distress amongst this target group.

The central focus of the Mellow campaign is the creation and strengthening of relationships between service users and staff working in mental health or related services. Their target group is men of African and African Caribbean backgrounds with mental health problems.

SERVICE DESCRIPTION

Mellow is a small team based in the NHS Trust's headquarters. They are not direct providers of front-line mental health services. Mellow facilitates and supports relationships to be built between individuals and services. They sometimes work with individuals, with groups or with large sections of the community to support relationship building with services.

APPROACH

Relying heavily on systemic approaches, Mellow seeks to interrupt belief systems. For example, staff express views about hopelessness or the perceived risk posed by African Caribbean service users. Individual service users and members of the local African and African Caribbean community express views about the coercive and untherapeutic approach of services. Mellow focuses on dialogue, analysing it and encouraging clarity and honesty. Mellow is increasingly using the appreciate inquiry approach (Cooperrider and Srivasta 1987). This approach begins with the identification of the matter on which the inquiry focuses. Appreciate inquiry starts from what works well and recognises that organisations spend a disproportionate amount of time focusing on what does not work well at the expense of learning from what does.

HOW IT LOOKS IN PRACTICE

Mellow has used different systems of delivery. For example, one project included the use of drama productions as an educational tool for mental health staff. The content of these productions were service user accounts of experience in services. Service users delivered the dramatic pieces. This was a powerful way of opening up dialogue between service users and workers.

Another Mellow project (Alternative Pathways) focused on identifying a cohort of 18 service users who had inpatient detentions. The project worked with staff, service users and carers to review pathways through services and to try to identify variables that may have consistently contributed to the given outcomes. The aim was to consider whether alternative action at different times could have led to different outcomes.

JUDGING THE SUCCESS OF MELLOW

The overall aims are broad (i.e. to reduce the over-representation of African and African Caribbean men in East London Mental Health Services) and success at the strategic level is difficult to attribute to Mellow. A change or static position in the service outcomes could indicate an impact elsewhere in the system. It is easier to identify the successes in relation to the subordinate aim (the local critical success factors) which is the improvement of engagement between workers and service users from African and African Caribbean backgrounds.

Each project within Mellow is evaluated often through seeking feedback from the service users and the staff involved. Service users report their satisfaction and staff report being challenged to reflect on their practice. Mellow reports having successful delivery of the process factors that are key to ensuring positive outcomes. More research is required to enable causal links to be identified despite the challenge of teasing these out from the multiple variables and the interactions between them.

Changing Outcomes, Camden and Islington NHS Foundation Trust

Changing Outcomes is currently being implemented. It is included as an example of trying to establish a causal relationship between service inputs and service user outcomes.

AIMS

Changing Outcomes strives towards the following outcomes:

- a reduction in the number of people from African and African Caribbean backgrounds admitted to psychiatric intensive care units

- a reduction in the number of people admitted under section 3 of the Mental Health Act 1983

- a reduction in the proportion of people readmitted within 120 days.

DESCRIPTION

Changing Outcomes is an approach rather than a service. It is based on the principle of beginning with the end in mind (Covey 1989). Team and delivery systems set targets for closing the gap on variations in service utilisation by people of African and African Caribbean backgrounds. The term 'delivery systems' relates to a network of sector-based services that have an interdependent impact on outcomes. For example, use of psychiatric intensive care units (PICUs) may be affected by the actions of both the community mental health team and the acute psychiatric wards. Length of stay may be affected by the decisions of inpatient staff but also by the responsiveness of community staff to enable discharge.

APPROACH

Changing Outcomes therefore has no staff team but is an approach throughout the organisation based on three principles:

- Begin with the end in mind – identify what needs to change and set targets.

- Make a working assumption that services have the ability to help change outcomes for African and African Caribbean people.

- Invest in the possibility that the relationship between worker and service user is the primary vehicle for change (where pharmacology and other models of intervention have failed).

HOW IT WILL LOOK IN PRACTICE

Workers will prioritise the relationship with African and African Caribbean service users as a medium for change. Counselling skills will be used to explore underlying thoughts, feelings and concerns of the service user. The relationship will not on its own be expected to deliver all change required but its strength will lead to increased opportunity to incorporate interventions such as counselling and psychotherapy and access to meaningful daytime activity. Explanatory models will inform practice (Kleinman and Benson 2006). Where a service user has been in the system for a long time the worker will still invest in exploring the service user's own perspective on his or her mental health problems in line with the government's policy direction (Department of Health 2007d). Seeking understanding will not be restricted just to mental health problems. The concerns of the service user, including the impact of race and racism, will be explored. This will require teams and sectors to agree to prioritise the effort put into working with service users from African and African Caribbean backgrounds. This will utilise the risk-based approach to recognise that without some mitigation certain segments of the service user base are likely to experience more aversive aspects of mental health services.

JUDGING THE SUCCESS OF CHANGING OUTCOMES

Success of the approach will be measured by achievement of targets agreed by delivery systems. Each sector team will have agreed targets, developed with service users. These will be specific, such as:

- 5 per cent reduction in the use of PICU by African and African Caribbean people measured by number of admissions as a proportion of all admissions

- 5 per cent reduction in repeat admissions by African Caribbean people as a proportion of all repeat admissions (this will rely on using standard agreed definitions of repeat admissions and procedures for monitoring these).

Because of the sector-based approach, Changing Outcomes will enable workers to have more confidence in attributing success to a causal link. The adoption of a clearly identifiable critical process (or effort) factor will assist in narrowing the possibilities of variables to be considered in any evaluation of success.

Antenna Assertive Outreach, Barnet, Enfield and Haringey NHS Trust

Aims

This service aims to achieve engagement of African and African Caribbean people in statutory mental health services.

SERVICE DESCRIPTION

Antenna is configured as an assertive outreach team for young people. The team includes traditional professional roles such as consultant psychiatrist and psychologist. There is priority on having members of the team with competence in youth work. They employ a specific carer support worker.

APPROACH

Antenna operates within a statutory mental health service and sees its priority as diverting people away from these and towards generic services. There are two key aspects to their approach. The first is social marketing, which is based on segmenting the potential mental health service user base and utilising bespoke techniques to attract young African and African Caribbean people. Antenna also recognises that services traditionally save their best work until the service user's need and presentation are at their most acute. Their approach is to invest in creative ways to engage service users, meeting them at their preferred place or activity provided there are no prohibitive factors such as the content of the service's risk assessment.

Antenna's reliance on services outside traditional mental health services has led them to develop 'quality circles'. These are networks of services that have been approved as providers of services that are consistent with the philosophy and practice of Antenna. This Antenna 'kite mark' is achieved through an assessment and recognises that they are an approved provider of the investment to close competency gaps, for example through training.

Antenna works with families as partners in support of young people using the service.

HOW IT LOOKS IN PRACTICE

Antenna provides a mix of traditional statutory mental health service functions such as a psychiatric assessment and youth work. These are integrated into a single approach. The consultant psychiatrist may undertake an assessment during a game of pool. Sport is a key medium through which engagement is achieved but other activities such as applying for places to pursue further or higher education are also utilised.

Carers (usually parents) of the young people are supported through reviews and support. Information packs are provided about the services offered by Antenna as well as other services available. The documents produced by Antenna are designed to be attractive to young African and African Caribbean people.

In line with traditional assertive outreach models, Antenna works as a team on problem-solving with every service user. This enables the full spectrum of knowledge and skills of the team to be available to every service user.

JUDGING THE SUCCESS OF ANTENNA

Antenna was reviewed in *Out of the Maze* (Sainsbury Centre for Mental Health 2002b). The purpose of the document was to highlight a number of services that had achieved engagement with services users where others had failed. Antenna was cited as having achieved this.

The service itself has a target of establishing a relationship with the service user within the first six contacts. Engagement is determined by a willingness of the individual to work with the service to try to address issues of concern. Achievement of this is used to judge the extent of service success. The service user outcomes judged by improvements in quality of life. Plans are set with each individual and the extent to which these are achieved is monitored.

Conclusion

Each service considered in this chapter began with no 'rule book' but tried to develop an approach that promotes engagement with black service users. This is considered to be a means of working towards improved outcomes and less reliance on more restrictive aspects of mental health services. The engagement itself is not considered as the tool for change but the vehicle through which change and improvement can occur. As more positive examples of services are evaluated the closer mental health services will be to having evidence of not only the problems but also of the potential solutions to the disparities that exist.

CHAPTER 11

CONCLUSION

People from black and minority ethnic backgrounds experience racism and discrimination inside and outside of mental health services. Racism is intensely painful and has an adverse impact on the social, economic, psychological, physical and mental wellbeing of those who experience it. Very few people would argue otherwise.

The impact of people's circumstances on the precipitation, compounding or worsening of their mental health problems is acknowledged even by those who give biological factors primacy in arguments about causes.

Since the 1980s there have been several policies, reports and programmes of change to address the disparities for people from BME groups in mental health services. Still, few services can demonstrate that they are tackling these disparities in a way that is proportionate to the scale of disadvantage. Individual workers struggle to rank highly the risk of adverse outcomes for BME service users amongst those that determine the priorities in their practice. At the very least mental health services show disregard for those risks that affect people from BME groups, i.e. that they will have poorer experiences and poorer outcomes. It is not routine for practitioners to record as a risk that adverse outcomes will occur unless action is taken. Workers do not feel that they would be held to account if disparities persist whilst they have no evidence of plans to mitigate these. Complicity leaves mental health organisations in an indefensible position when faced with accusations of institutional racism meanwhile individual workers struggle with gaps in resources (including time), knowledge and skills to make a difference. Assumptions persist that workers are equipped to provide services that strive to reduce inequalities despite the lack of evidence to support this.

Practitioners and service providers need to deconstruct the key knowledge, skills and attitudes in working with BME service users with mental health problems. These need to be rebuilt with the capacity and capability to work effectively with difference. Practitioners need to be honest about their fears, likes and prejudices and find ways to ameliorate their effects. They need to learn how to deal with matters that make them uncomfortable, including talking about ethnicity, race and culture and challenging others about their oversights and discrimination.

Relationships between practitioners and service users from BME backgrounds are central to achieving change. These relationships are the carriers for change; the containers for all interventions provided by mental health practitioners. Collectively practitioners have not yet been able to utilise these relationships to achieve demonstrable improvements in outcomes for people from BME backgrounds. It is the author's intention that *Working with Ethnicity, Race and Culture in Mental Health* moves the agenda on from analysing the whys and wherefores of the persistence of disparities. In relation to practice that might change outcomes, it is hoped that it will go some way towards describing what 'good' looks like.

REFERENCES

Addis, M. and Mhalik, J. (2003) 'Men, masculinity and the contexts of help-seeking.' *American Psychologist 58*, 1, 5–14

Ahmad, A. (1990) *Back Perspectives in Social Work*. Birmingham: Venture Press.

Ahmad, W. (2000) *Ethnicity, Disability and Chronic Illness*. Buckinghamshire: Open University Press.

Alexander, P. (1987) *Racism, Resistance and Revolution*. London: Bookmarks.

Altman, N. (2006) 'Black and White Thinking: A Psychoanalyst Reconsiders Race.' In R. Moodley and S. Palmer (eds) *Race, Culture and Psychotherapy Critical Perspective in Multicultural Practice*. Sussex: Routledge.

Arnold, E. (2007) 'Separation and loss: The impact on the emotional health of Afro Caribbean young people *'Attachment: New Directions in Psychotherapy and Relational Psychoanalysis'* 1, 2, 213–220.

Audit Commission (2006) *Managing Finances in Mental Health. A Review to Support Improvement and Best Practice*. National Report. London: Audit Commission.

Audit Commission (2007) *Auditors' Local Evaluation 2007/08: Guidance for NHS Organisations*. Guidance. London: Audit Commission.

Baldwin, S. (1997). *Needs Assessment and Community Care: Clinical Practice and Policy Making*. Oxford: Butterworth-Heinemann.

Banfield, P. and Kay, R. (2008) *Introduction to Human Resource Management*. Oxford: Oxford University Press.

Banks, N. (2002a) 'What is a Positive Black identity?' In K. Dwived (ed.) *Meeting the Needs of Ethnic Minority Children*. London: Jessica Kingsley Publishers.

Banks, N. (2002b) 'Mixed-race Children and Families.' In K. Dwivedi, *Meeting the Needs of Ethnic Minority Children*. London: Jessica Kingsley Publishers.

Banton, M. (1965) *Roles: An Introduction to the Study of Social Relations*. London: Tavistock Publications Limited.

Banton, M. (1967) *Race Relations*. London: Tavistock Publications Limited.

Bennett, J., Kalathil, J. and Keating, F. (2007) *Race Equality Training in Mental Health Services in England: Does One Size Fit All?* London: Sainsbury Centre for Mental Health.

Beresford, P., Shamash, M., Forrest, V. and Turner, M. (2005) *Developing Social Care: Service Users' Vision for Adult Support*. London: Social Care Institute for Excellence.

Bhopal, R. (1997) 'Is research into ethnicity and health racist, unsound, or important science?' *British Medical Journal 314*, 1751.

Bhugra, D. (2002) 'Ethnic factors and service utilisation.' *Current Opinion in Psychiatry 15*, 201–204.

Bhugra, D. and Bhui, K. (2001) *Cross Cultural Psychiatry: A Practical Guide*. London: Arnold.

Bhugra, D. and Bhui, K. (2002) 'Racism in Psychiatry: Paradigm Lost–Paradigm Regained.' In K. Bhui (ed.) *Racism & Mental Health: Prejudice and Suffering*. London: Jessica Kingsley Publishers.

Bhugra, D., Harding, C. Lippett, R. (2004) 'Pathways into care and satisfaction with primary care for black patients in South London,' *Journal of Mental Health 13*, (2), 171–183.

Bhugra, D., Lippett, R. and Cole, E. (1999) 'Pathways into Care: An Explanation of the Factors that May Affect Minority Ethnic Groups.' In D. Bhugra and V. Bahl (eds) *Ethnicity: An Agenda for Mental Health*. London: Gaskell.

Bhui, K. (ed.) (2002) *Racism and Mental Health: Prejudice and Suffering*. London: Jessica Kingsley Publishers.

Bhui, K. and Bhugra, D. (2002) 'Explanatory models for mental distress: Implications for clinical practice and research.' *British Journal of Psychiatry 181*, 7–6.

Bhui, K. and Bhugra, D. (2004) 'Communication with patients from other cultures: The place of explanatory models.' *Advances in Psychiatric Treatment 10*, 474–478.

Bhui, K. and Sashidharan, S. (2003) 'Should there be separate psychiatric services for ethnic minority groups?' *British Journal of Psychiatry 182*, 10–12.

Bhui, K., Stansfeld, S., Hull, S., Priebe, S., Mole, F. and Feder, G. (2003) 'Ethnic variations in pathways to and use of specialist mental health services in the UK.' *British Journal of Psychiatry 182*, 105–116.

Blackman, L. (2001) *Hearing Voices: Embodiment and Experience*. London: Free Association Books.

Blackman, L. (2007) 'Psychiatric culture and bodies of resistance.' *Body and Society 13*, 2, 1–23.

Bloisi, W. (2006) *An Introduction to Human Resources Management*. Maidenhead: McGraw-Hill Higher Education.

Bloom, S. (1997) *Creating Sanctuary: Towards an Evaluation of Sane Societies*. London: Routledge.

Bond, M. and Holland, S. (1998) *Skills of Clinical Supervision for Nurses*. Buckingham: Open University Press.

Bowl, R. (2007a) 'The need for change in UK mental health services: South Asian service users' views.' *Ethnicity and Health 12*, 1, 1–19.

Bowl, R. (2007b) 'Responding to ethnic diversity: Black service users' views of mental health services in the UK.' *Diversity in Health and Social Care 4*, 201–210.

Brett, J., Behfar, K. and Kern, M. (2006) 'Managing multicultural teams.' Harvard *Business Review*, November, 84–91.

Burnard, P. (2005) *Counselling Skills for Health Professionals*. Cheltenham: Nelson Thornes Limited.

Callan, A. and Littlewood, R. (1998) 'Patient satisfaction: Ethnic origin or explanatory model?' *International Journal of Social Psychiatry 44*, 1–11.

Canales, G. (2000) 'Gender as Subculture: The First Division of Multicultural Diversity.' In I. Cuellar and F. Paniagua (eds) *Handbook of Multicultural Health: Assessment and Treatment of Diverse Populations*. San Diego, CA: Academic Press.

Carmichael, S. and Hamilton, C. (1967) *Black Power: The Politics of Liberation in America*. New York: Vintage Books.

Cashmore, E. and Troyna, B. (1990) *Introduction to Race Relations*. Hampshire: The Falmer Press.

Chakraborty, A. and McKenzie, K. (2002) 'Does racial discrimination cause mental illness?' *British Journal of Psychiatry 180*, 475–477.

Chantler, K. (2002) 'The invisibility of black women in mental health services.' *The Mental Health Review 7*, 1, 22–24.

Collin, A. (2007) 'Learning and Development.' In J. Beardwell and T. Claydon (eds) *Human Resources Management: A Contemporary Approach.* Essex: Financial Times/ Prentice Hall.

Commission for Healthcare Audit and Inspection (2007a) *Count Me In 2007: Results of the 2007 National Census of Inpatients in Mental Health and Learning Disability Services in England and Wales.* London: CHAI.

Commission for Healthcare Audit and Inspection (2007b) *Healthcare Watchdog to Review Race Equality in NHS Trusts.* Press Release. 22 November.

Commission for Racial Equality (2007) *A Lot Done, A Lot To Do.* London: CRE.

Community Care Magazine (2006) 'Timid mental health bodies criticised.' 2 February.

Cooper, C., Morgan, C., Byrne, M., Dazzan, P. *et al.* (2008) 'Perceptions of disadvantage, ethnicity and psychosis.' *British Journal of Psychiatry 192*, 18596190.

Cooper, L., Beach, M., Johnson, R. and Inui, T. (2006) 'Understanding how race and ethnicity influence relationships in health care.' *Journal of General Internal Medicine 21*, S21–S27.

Cooperrider, D. and Srivastva, S. (1987) 'Appreciative inquiry in organizational Life.' *Research in Organizational Change and Development 1*, 129–169.

Covey, S. (1989) *The 7 Habits of Highly Effective People: Powerful Lessons in Personal Change.* New York: Fireside.

Coyte, M.; Gilbert, P. and Nichols, V. (2007) *Spirituality, Values and Mental Health: Jewels for the Journey.* London: Jessica Kingsley Publishers.

Crawford, J., Nobles, W. and Leary, J. (2003) 'Repatriations and Healthcare for African Americans: Repairing the Damage from the Legacy of Slavery.' In R. Windrush (ed.) *Should America Pay: Slavery and the Raging Debate on Repatriations.* New York: HarperCollins Publishing Inc.

Curry, A. (1964) 'Myths, transference and the black psychotherapist.' *International Review of Psychoanalysis 45*, 7–17.

David, S. and Knight, B. (2008) 'Stress and coping among gay men: Age and ethnic differences.' *Psychology and Ageing 23*, 1, 62–69.

Davidson, C. (1985) 'The Theoretical Antecedents to Interpersonal Skills Training.' In C. Kagan (ed.) *Interpersonal Skills in Nursing.* Kent: Croom Helm Limited.

Davis, B., Bebbington, A. and Charnley, H. (1990) *Resources, Needs and Outcomes in Community-Based Care.* Hertfordshire: Gower Publishing Company Limited.

Davis, S. (2007) Racism as trauma: Some reflections on psychotherapeutic work with clients from the African Caribbean Diaspora from an attachment based perspective. *Attachment: New Directions in Psychotherapy and Relational Psychoanalysis 1*, 2, 179–199.

Dein, K., Williams, P. and Dein, S. (2007) 'Ethnic bias in the application of the Mental Health Act 1983.' *Advances in Psychiatric Treatment 13*, 350–357.

Department for Education and Skills (2006) *Care Matters: Transforming the Lives of Children and Young People.* London: DFES.

Department of Health (1996) *Beyond the Boundary: An Action Guide for Health Service Purchasers – Consultation and Involvement.* Leeds: DoH NHS Ethnic Health Unit.

Department of Health (1998) A *First Class Service: Quality in the New NHS.* Policy. London: DoH.

Department of Health (1999) *National Service Framework for Mental Health: Modern Standards and Service Models.* London: DoH.

Department of Health (2002a) *Women's Mental Health: Into the Mainstream: Strategic Development of Mental Healthcare for Women.* Consultation. London: DoH.

Department of Health (2002b) National *Suicide Prevention Strategy for England.* Policy. London. DoH.

Department of Health (2003a) *Into the Mainstream: Analysis of the responses to the consultation document.* London: DoH.

Department of Health (2003b) *Mainstreaming Gender and Women's Health* Implementation Guidance. London: DoH.

Department of Health (2003c) *Inside Outside: Improving Mental Health for Black and Minority Communities in England.* London: DoH.

Department of Health (2003d) Inspiring Hope: Recognising the Importance of Spirituality in a Whole Person Approach to Mental Health. London: DoH.

Department of Health (2004a) *Emerging Best Practices in Mental Health Recovery.* Guidance. London: DoH.

Department of Health (2004b) *The NHS Knowledge and Skills Framework (NHS KSF) and the Development Review.'* Policy. London: DoH.

Department of Health (2004c) *Standards for Better Health.* Policy. London: DoH.

Department of Health (2004d) *The National Service Framework for Mental Health: Five Years On.* London: DoH.

Department of Health (2005a) *A Practical Guide to Ethnic Monitoring in the NHS and Social Care.* London: DoH.

Department of Health (2005b) *Delivering Race Equality in Mental Health Care: An Action Plan for Reform Inside and Outside Services and the Government's Response to the Death of David Bennett.* London: DoH.

Department of Health (2005c) *Guiding Statement on Recovery Guidance.* London: DoH.

Department of Health (2006) *Our Health Our Care Our Say: A New Direction for Community Services.* Command Paper. London: DoH.

Department of Health (2007a) *Best Practice in Managing Risk.* Best Practice Guidance. London: DoH.

Department of Health (2007b) *Ten Essential Shared Capabilities: Race Equality and Cultural Capability.* www.lincoln.ac.uk/ccawi/esc/esc_web/assets/mod5_home.html

Department of Health (2007c) *Lesbian, Gay and Bisexual People from Black and Minority Ethnic Communities.* Briefing. London: DoH.

Department of Health (2007d) *Consultation on Guidance on 'Finding a Shared Vision of How People's Mental Health Problems Should Be Understood'.* Consultation. London: DoH.

Department of Health (2008a) *A Consultation on the Framework for the Registration of Health and Social Care Providers.* Consultation. London: DoH.

Department of Health (2008b) *Transforming Social Care.* Circular. London: DoH.

Desai, S. (2006) 'Accounting for difference: Analysis of nine murder inquiry reports involving black people with mental health problems.' *Diversity in Health and Social Care 3,* 203–210.

DeSisto, M., Harding, C., McCormick, R., Ashikaga, T. and Brooks, G. (1995) 'The Maine and Vermont three-decade studies of serious mental illness: II. longitudinal course comparisons.' *British Journal of Psychiatry 167,* 3, 338–342.

Dewar, B. and Sharp, C. (2006) 'Using evidence: How action learning can support individual and organisation learning through action research/' *Educational Action Research 14,* 2, 219–237.

Dominelli, L. (1992) 'An Uncaring Profession?' In P. Braham, A. Rattansi and R. Skellington (eds) *Racism and Antiracism: Inequalities, Opportunities and Policies.* London: Sage Publications Ltd.

Elze, D. (2002) 'Risk factors for internalizing and externalizing problems among gay, lesbian and bisexual adolescents.' *Social Work Research 26,* 2, 89–99.

Equalities Act (2006) London: HMSO.

Evans, S., Huxley, P., Gatly, C., Webber, M., et al. (2006) 'Mental health, burnout and job satisfaction among social workers in England and Wales.' *British Journal of Psychiatry 188*, 75–80.

Evening Standard, The (2005) 'Panel that freed the Camden *Ripper is Criticised.' 20 September, p.7.*

Fairbairn, A. (2007) 'Payment by results in mental health: The current state of play in England.' *Advances in Psychiatric Treatment 13*, 3–6.

Fanon, F. (1967) *Black Skin, White Masks.* London: Pluto Press.

Faulkner, A. (1985) 'The Organisational Context of Interpersonal Skills in Nursing.' In C. Kagan (ed.) *Interpersonal Skills in Nursing.* Kent: Croom Helm Limited.

Feifel, H. (1958) 'Symposium on relationships between religion and mental health: Introductory remarks.' *American Psychologist 13*, 10, 565–566.

Fernando, S. (1991) *Mental Health, Race and Culture.* Hampshire: Macmillan Press.

Fernando, S. (ed.) (1995) *Mental Health in a Multi-ethnic Society: A Multi-disciplinary Handbook.* London: Routledge.

Fernando, S., Ndegwa, D. and Wilson, M. (1998) *Forensic Psychiatry, Race and Culture.* London: Routledge.

Fernando, S. (2005) 'Multicultural mental health services: Projects for minority ethnic communities in England.' *Transcultural Psychiatry 42*, 3, 420–436.

Ferns, P. (2007) 'Race Equality and Cultural Capability.' In T. Stickley and T. Basset (eds) *Teaching Mental Health.* Sussex: John Wiley and Sons Limited.

Freeman, H. (2003) 'Racial discrimination and mental illness.' *British Journal of Psychiatry 182*, 77–79.

Fry, H., Ketteridge, S. and Marshall, S. (2000) *A Handbook for Teaching and Learning in Higher Education.* London: Kogan Page.

Fryer, P. (1984) *Staying Power: The History of Black People in Britain.* London: Pluto Press.

Gilbert, P. (2005) *Leadership: Being Effective and Remaining Human.* Dorset: Russell House Publishing.

Green, G., Bradby, H., Chan, A., Lee, M. and Eldridge, K. (2002) 'Is the English National Health Service meeting the needs of mentally distressed Chinese women?' *Journal of Health Services Research and Policy 7*, 4, 26–221.

Greene, B. (2006) 'African-American Lesbians and Gay Men in Psychodynamic Psychotherapies?' In R. Moodley and S. Palmer (eds) *Race, Culture and Psychotherapy. Critical Perspectives in Multicultural Practice.* Sussex: Routledge.

Griffith, M. (1977) 'The influence of race on the psychotherapeutic relationship.' *Psychiatry 40*, 279640.

Griffiths, S. (1992) 'The neglected male.' *British Journal of Hospital Medicine 48*, 627–629.

Guardian, The (1987) 'Is racism driving blacks out of their minds?' 30 September, 27.

Guardian, The (2004) 'NHS Urged to Combat Institutional Racism. 12 February. www.guardian.co.uk/society/2004/feb/12/mentalhealth.raceintheuk2

Guardian, The (2005) 'NHS "not institutionally racist" 11 January. www.guardian.co.uk/society/2005/jan/11/mentalhealth.politics1

Hall, S. (1996) New Ethnicities. In D. Morley and K. Chen (eds) *Stuart Hall: Critical Dialogues in Cultural Studies.* London: Routledge.

Handy, C. (1985) *Understanding Organizations.* Middlesex: Penguin Books Limited.

Hardy, A., Fowler, D., Freeman, D. and Smith, B. (2005) 'Trauma and hallucinatory experience in psychosis.' *Journal of Nervous and Mental Disease 193*, 501–507.

Harrison, G., Owens, D., Holton, A., Neilson, D. and Boot, D. (1988) 'A prospective study of severe mental disorder in Afro-Caribbean patients.' *Psychological Medicine 18*, 643–657.

Harrison, P. (2007) 'Holistic thinking and integrated care: Working with black and minority ethnic individuals and communities in health and social care.' *Journal of Integrated Care 15*, 3, 3–6.

Hellman, R. and Klein, E. (2004) 'A program for lesbian, gay, bisexual and transgender individuals with major mental illnesses.' *Journal of Gay and Lesbian Psychotherapy 8*, 3/4, 67–82.

Hilton, C., Ghaznavi, F. and Zuberi, T. (2002) 'Religious beliefs and practices in acute mental health patients.' *Nursing Standard 16*, 38, 33–36.

Holland, S. (1995) 'Interaction in Women's Mental Health and Neighbourhood Developments.' In S. Fernando (ed.) *Mental Health in a Multi-ethnic Society*. London: Routledge.

Ingram, D. (1999) 'Same gender sexually active Black/ African women: Sexual identities, sexual orientation, coping styles and depression.' *The Sciences and Engineering 60*, 2, 831.

Jackson, J. and Brown, L. (1996) 'Lesbians of African Heritage: Coming out in the straight community.' *Journal of Gay and Lesbian Social Services 5*, 4, 53–67.

Jewson, N. and Mason, D. (1992) 'The Theory and Practice of Equal Opportunities Policies: Liberal and Radical Approaches.' In P. Braham, A. Rattansi and R. Skellington (eds) *Racism and Antiracism: Inequalities, Opportunities and Policies*. London: Sage Publications Ltd.

Jones, H., Cross, W. and DeFour, D. (2007) 'Race-related stress, racial identity attitudes and mental health among black women.' *Journal of Black Psychology 33*, 2, 208–231.

Joseph, J. (2003) *The Gene Illusion: Genetic Research in Psychiatry and Psychology Under the Microscope*. Ross-on-Wye: PCCS Books.

Kareem, J. and Littlewood, R. (eds) (1992) *Intercultural Therapy: Themes, Interpretations and Practice*. Oxford: Blackwell Science Limited.

Karlsen, S., Nazroo, J., McKenzie, K., Bhui, K. and Weich, S. (2005) 'Racism, psychosis and common mental disorder among ethnic minority groups in England.' *Psychological Medicine 35*, 1795–1803.

Katz, I. (1996) *The Construction of Racial Identity in Children of Mixed Parentage: Mixed Metaphors*. London: Jessica Kingsley Publishers.

Keating, F., Robertson, D. and Kotecha, N. (2003) *Ethnic Diversity and Mental Health in London*: Recent Developments. London: Kings Fund.

Kent, B. (2004) *Performance Management*. Gloucestershire: Management Books 2000 Ltd.

Kikkert, M., Schene, A., Koeter, M. Robson, D. (2006) 'Medication adherence in schizophrenia: Exploring patients', carers' and professionals' views.' *Schizophrenia Bulletin 32*, 4, 786–794.

Killaspy, H., Bebbington, P., Blizard, R., Johnson, S. *et al*. (2006) 'The REACT study: Randomised evaluation of assertive community treatment in north London.' *British Medical Journal 332*, 815–820.

King, M., McKeown, E., Warner, J. Ramsey, A. *et al*. (2003) *Mental Health and Social Wellbeing of Gay Men, Lesbians and Bisexuals in England and Wales: A Summary of Findings*. London: Mind.

Kleinman, A. and Benson, P. (2006) 'Anthropology in the clinic: The problem of cultural competency and how to fix it.' *PLoS Medicine 3*, 10, 1673–1676.

Kolb, D. (1984) *Experiential Learning Experience as the Source of Learning and Development*. Englewood Cliffs, NJ: Financial Times/Prentice Hall.

Konik, J. and Stewart, A. (2004) 'Sexual identity development in the context of compulsory heterosexuality.' *Journal of Personality 72*, 4, 815–844.

Langan, J. and Lindow, V. (2004) *Living with Risk: Mental Health Service User Involvement in Risk Assessment and Management*. York: Joseph Rowntree Foundation.

Lapakko, D. (1997) 'Three cheers for language: A closer examination of a widely cited study.' *Communication Education 46*, 63–67.

Lawrence, E., Shaw, P., Baker, D., Baron-Cohen, S. and David, A. (2004) 'Measuring empathy: Reliability and validity of the empathy quotient.' *Psychological Medicine 34*, 911–924.

Leary, K. (2006) 'The John Bowlby Memorial Lecture 2005: How Race is Lived in the Consulting Room.' In K. White (ed.) *Unmasking Race, Culture and Attachment in the Psychoanalytic Space*. London: H. Karnac (Books) Limited.

Leigh, A. and Maynard, M. (2002) *Leading Your Team: How to Involve and Inspire Teams (People Skills for Professionals)*. London: Nicholas Brealey Publishing Limited.

Levine, P. (1997) *Waking the Tiger: Healing Trauma*, Bekerly, CA: North Atlantic Books.

Lewis, L. (2006) 'Sex and Sexuality.' In L. Lewis and R. Mcanulty (eds) *Sexuality Today: Trends and Controversies*. CT: Praeger Publishers.

Liggan, D. and Kay, J. (2006) 'Race in the Room: Issues in the Dynamic Psychotherapy of African-Americans.' In R. Moodley and S. Palmer (eds) *Race, Culture and Psychotherapy: Critical Perspectives in Multicultural Practice*. Sussex: Routledge.

Littlewood, R., Jadhav, S. and Ryder, A. (2007) 'A cross-national study of stigmatization of severe psychiatric illness: Historical review, methodological considerations and development of the questionnaire.' *Transcultural Psychiatry 44*: 171.

Lousada, J. (2000) 'The state of mind we are in.' *British Journal of Psychotherapy 16*, 4, 467–476.

Littlewood, R. and Lipsedge, M. (1989) *Aliens and Alienists: Ethnic Minorities and Psychiatry*. London: Unwin Hyman.

MacPherson, W. (1999) *The Stephen Lawrence Inquiry*. London: HMSO.

McAuley, C. and Young, C. (2006) 'The mental health of looked after children: Challenges for CAMHS provision.' *Journal of Social Work Practice 20*, 1, 91–103.

McCabe, R. and Priebe, S. (2004) 'Explanatory models of illness in schizophrenia: comparison of four ethnic groups.' *British Journal of Psychiatry 185*, 25–30.

McGrath, J. and Emmerson, W.B. (1999) 'Treatment of schizophrenia.' *British Medical Journal 319*, 7216, 1045–1048.

McKenzie, K. (2001) 'Comparison of the outcome and treatment of psychosis in people of Caribbean origin living in the UK and British whites.' *British Journal of Psychiatry 178*, 160–165.

McKenzie, K. and Bhui, K. (2007) 'Institutional racism in mental health care.' *British Medical Journal 334*, 649–650.

McKenzie, K. and Chakraborty, A. (2003) 'Racial discrimination and mental illness.' *British Journal of Psychiatry 182*, 77–79.

McKenzie, K., Serfaty, M. and Crawford, M. (2003) 'Suicide in ethnic minority groups.' *British Journal of Psychiatry 183*, 2, 100–101.

McLean, C., Campbell, C. and Cornish, F. (2003) 'African Caribbean interactions with mental health services in the UK: Experiences and expectations of exclusion as (re)productive of health inequalities.' *Social Science and Medicine 56*, 657–669.

Mearns, D. and Thorne, B. (1988) *Person-centred Counselling in Action*. London: Sage Publications Limited.

Mehra, H. (2002) 'Residential Care for Ethnic Minority Children.' In K. Dwivedi (ed.) *Meeting The Needs of Ethnic Minority Children* London: Jessica Kingsley Publishers.

Mehrabian, A. and Ferris, S. (1967) 'Inference of attitudes from nonverbal communication in two channels'. *Journal of Consulting Psychology 31*, 3, 248–252.

Mental Health Act Commission (2006) *Count Me In: The National Mental Health and Ethnicity Census: 2005 Service User Survey.* London: MHAC.

Mental Health Act Commission (2008) *Risks, Rights, Recovery: Twelfth Biennial Report 2005–2007.* London: MHAC.

Miller, R., Williams, G. and Hayashi, A. (2007) *The 5 Paths to Persuasion: The Art of Selling Your Message.* London: Kogan Page Limited.

Mind (2007) *Another Assault: Mind's Campaign for Equal Access to Justice for People with Mental Health Problems.* London: Mind.

Minnis, H., McMillan, A., Gilles, M. and Smith, S. (2001) 'Racial stereotyping: Survey of psychiatrists in the United Kingdom.' *British Medical Journal 323*, 905–906.

Miranda, J., Bernal, G., Lau, A., Khon, L., Hwang, W. and La Framboise, T. (2005) 'State of science on psychosocial interventions for ethnic minorities.' *Annual Review of Clinical Psychology 1*, 11396142.

Modood, T., Berthoud, R., Lakey, J., Nazroo, J. *et al.* (1998) Ethnic *Minorities in Britain: Diversity and Disadvantage.* London: Policy Studies Institute.

Mohan, R., McCrone, P., Szmukler, G., Micali, N., Afuwape, S. and Thornicroft, G. (2006) 'Ethnic differences in mental health service use among patients with psychotic disorders.' *Social Psychiatry and Psychiatric Epidemiology 41*, 771–776.

Montgomery, J. (2005) *Preliminary Model for Understanding and Healing the Impact of Slavery on American Women of African Descent.* CA: The Wright Institute.

Moodley, R. and Palmer, S. (eds) (2006) *Race, Culture and Psychotherapy: Critical Perspective in Multicultural Practice.* Sussex: Routledge.

Morgan, C., Mallet, R., Hutchinson, G., Bagalkote, H., Morgan, K., Fearon, P., Dazan, P., Boydell, J., McKenzie, K., Harrson, G., Murray, R., Jones, P., Craig, T. and Leff, J. (2005a) 'Pathways to care and ethnicity 1: Sample characteristics and compulsory admission.' *British Journal of Psychiatry 186*, 281–289.

Morgan, C., Mallet, R., Hutchinson, G., Bagalkote, H., Morgan, K., Fearon, P., Dazan, P., Boydell, J., McKenzie, K., Harrison, G., Murray, R., Jones, P., Craig, T. and Leff, J. (2005b) 'Pathways to care and ethnicity 2: Source of referral and help seeking.' *British Journal of Psychiatry 186*, 290–296.

Morris, J. (2004a) *People with Physical Impairments and Mental Health Support Needs: A Critical Review of the Literature.* York: Joseph Rowntree Foundation.

Morris, J. (2004b) *One Town for My Body, Another for My Mind: Services for People with Physical Impairments and Mental Health Support Needs.* York: Joseph Rowntree Foundation.

Newbigging, K., McKeown, M., Habte-Mariam, Z., Mullings, D., Jaye-Charles, J. and Holt, K. (2008) *Resource Guide 10: Commissioning and Providing Mental Health Advocacy for African and Caribbean Men.* London: Social Care Institute for Excellence.

NSCSTHA (2003) *Independent Inquiry into the Death of David Bennett.* London: Norfolk, Suffolk and Cambridgeshire Strategic Health Authority.

Office of the Deputy Prime Minister (2004) *Mental Health and Social Exclusion: Social Exclusion Unit Report.* London: OPDM.

Okitikpi, T. (1999) 'Children of mixed parentage in care: Why such a high number?' *Child Care in Practice 5*, 4, 396–405.

Okitikpi, T. (2005a) (ed.) *Working with Children of Mixed Parentage.* Dorset: Russell House Publishing.

Okitikpi, T. (2005b) 'Identity and identification: How mixed race parentage children adapt to a binary world.' In Okitikpi (ed.) *Working with Children of Mixed Parentage*. Dorset: Russell House Publishing.

Owen, J. (2006) *How to Manage*. Harlow: Prentice Hall.

Owusu-Bempah, K. (2005) 'Mulatto, Marginal Man, Half-Caste, Mixed-Race: The One Drop Rule in Professional Practice.' In T. Okitikpi (ed.) *Working with Children of Mixed Parentage*. Dorset: Russell House Publishing.

Parkman, S., Davies, S., Leese, M. and Phelan., M. Thornicroft, G. (1997) 'Ethnic Differences in Satisfaction with Mental Health Services Among Representative People with Psychosis in South London: PRiSM Study 4.' *British Journal of Psychiatry 171*, 260–264.

Peters, T. and Waterman, R. (1992) *In Search of Excellence*. New York: Harper and Row.

Quinn, A. (2007) 'Reflection on intergenerational trauma: Healing as a critical intervention.' *First Peoples Child and Family Review 3*, 4, 72–82.

Race Relations (Amendment) Act (2000) London: HMSO.

Rack, P. (1982) *Race, Culture and Mental Disorder*. London. Tavistock Routledge.

Raleigh, V., Irons, R., Hawe, E., Scobie, S., Cooke, A., Reeves, R., Petruckevich, A. and Harrison, J. (2007) 'Ethnic variations in the experience of mental health service users in England.' *British Journal of Psychiatry 191*, 304–312.

Razzano, L., Cook, J., Hamilton, M., Hughes, T. and Matthews, A. (2006) 'Predictors of mental health service use among lesbian and heterosexual women.' *Psychiatric Rehabilitation Journal 29*, 4, 289–298.

Read, J. (1997) 'Child abuse and psychosis: A literature review and implications for professional practice.' *Professional Psychology: Research and Practice 28*, 5, 448–456.

Read, J., Mosher, L.R. and Bentall, R.P. (eds) (2004) *Models of Madness: Psychological, Social and Biological Approaches to Schizophrenia*. Sussex: Brunner-Routledge.

Read, J., Perry, B., Moskowitz, A. and Connolly, J. (2001) 'The contribution of early traumatic events to schizophrenia in some patients: A traumagenic neurodevelopmental model.' *Psychiatry 64*, 319–345.

Read, J., Rudegair, T., Farrely, S. (2006) 'The Relationship Between Child Abuse and Psychosis: Public Opinion, Evidence, Pathways and Implications.' In W. Larkin and A. Morrison (eds) *Trauma and Psychosis*. London: Brunner-Routledge.

Read, J., Van Os, J., Morrison, A.P. and Ross, C.A. (2005) 'Childhood trauma, psychosis and schizophrenia: A literature review with theoretical and clinical implications.' *Acta Psychiatrica Scandinavica 112*, 330–350.

Read, M., Hammersley, P. and Rudegeair, T. (2007) 'Why, when and how to ask about childhood abuse.' *Advances in Psychiatric Treatment 13*, 101–110.

Reid, A. and Barrington, H. (1999) *Training Interventions: Promoting Learning Opportunities*. London: CIPD.

Ritchie, J., Dick, D. and Lingham, R. (1994) *The Report into the Care and Treatment of Christopher Clunis*. London: HMSO.

Robinson, L. (1995) *Psychology for Social Workers: Black Perspectives*. London: Routledge.

Robinson, L. (2005) 'Practice Issues: Working With Children of Mixed Parentage.' In T. Okitikpi (ed.) *Working with Children of Mixed Parentage*. Dorset: Russell House Publishing.

Romme, M. and Escher, S. (1993) *Accepting Voices*. London: Mind Publications.

Rothschild, B. (2000) *The Body Remembers: The Psychophysiology of Trauma*. New York: Norton.

Rubino, M. (2001) 'Psychologists clinical judgments about a female client with a visible disability, hidden disability or no disability.' *The Sciences and Engineering 62*, 3, 1596.

Sainsbury Centre for Mental Health (2002a) *Breaking The Circles of Fear: A Review of the Relationship Between Mental Health Services and African Caribbean Communities.* London: SCMH.

Sainsbury Centre for Mental Health (2002b) *Out of the Maze.* London: SCMH.

Sainsbury Centre for Mental Health (2004) *Payment by Results: What Does it Mean for Mental Health?* Policy Paper. London: SCMH.

Sainsbury Centre for Mental Health (2006) *The Cost of Race Inequality: Policy Paper No 6.* London: SCMH.

Sainsbury Centre for Mental Health (2007) *Reviewing the Care Programme Approach (CPA): A response from the Sainsbury Centre for Mental Health.* London: SCMH.

Sanderson, H., Thompson, J. and Kilbane, J. (2006) 'The emergence of person-centred planning as evidence-based practice.' *Journal of Integrated Care 14*, 2, 18–25.

Scheyett, A. and McCarthy, E. (2006) 'Women and men with mental illnesses: voicing different service needs.' *Journal of Women and Social Work 21*, 4, 40796418.

Scragg, T. (2001) *Managing at the Frontline: A Handbook for Managers in Social Care Agencies.* Brighton: Pavillion.

Sellers, R., Caldwell, C., Schmeelk-Cone, K. and Zimmerman, M. (2003) 'Racial identity, racial discrimination, perceived stress, and psychological distress among African American young adults.' *Journal of Health and Social Behavior 44*, 3, 302–317.

Senior, P. and Bhopal, R. (1994) 'Ethnicity as a variable in epidemiological research.' *British Medical Journal 309*, 327–330.

Sewell, H. (2004) 'Black and Minority Ethnic Groups.' In D. Duffy and T. Ryan (eds) *New Approaches to Preventing Suicide: A Manual for Practitioners.* London: Jessica Kingsley Publishers.

Shapiro, D.A. and Shapiro, D. (1982) 'Meta-analysis of comparative therapy outcome studies: A replication and refinement.' *Psychological Bulletin 92*, 581–604.

Silove, D., Sinnerbrink, I., Field, A., Manicavasagar, V. and Steel, Z. (1997) 'Anxiety, depression and PTSD in asylum-seekers: Associations with pre-migration trauma and post-migration stressors.' *British Journal of Psychiatry 170*, 351–357.

Singer, I. (2006) 'Unmasking Difference, Culture and Attachment in the Psychoanalytic Space.' In K. White (ed.) *Unmasking Race, Culture and Attachment in the Psychoanalytic Space.* London: H. Karnac (Books) Limited.

Singh, S. and Burns, T. (2006) 'Race and mental health: There is more to race than racism.' *British Medical Journal 333*, 64896651.

Singh, S., Greenwood, N., White, S. and Churchill, R. (2007) 'Ethnicity and the Mental Health Act 1983.' *British Journal of Psychiatry 191*, 99–105.

Slade, M. and Priebe, S. (2001) 'Are randomised controlled trials the only gold that glitters?' *British Journal of Psychiatry 179*, 286–287.

Social Care Institute for Excellence (2003) *Learning and Teaching in Social Work Education: Assessment.* Knowledge Review. London: SCIE.

Social Care Institute for Excellence (2004) *Learning Organisations: A Self Assessment Resource Pack.* London: SCIE.

Social Care Institute for Excellence (2007a) *A Common Purpose: Recovery in Future Mental Health Services.* Joint Position Paper 08. London: SCIE.

Social Care Institute for Excellence (2007b) *Practice Guide: The Participation of Adults, Including Older People, in Developing Social Care.* London: SCIE.

Spauwen, J., Krabbendam, L., Leib, R., Wittchen,H. and van Os, J. (2006) 'Impact of psychological drama on the development of psychotic symptoms: Relationship with psychotic proneness.' *British Journal of Psychiatry 188*, 527–533.

Sue, D.W. and Sue, D. (1990) *Counselling the Culturally Different.* New York: John Wiley and Sons.

Tan, R. (2006) 'Racism and Similarity: Paranoid-schizoid Restructures Revisited. In R. Moodley and S. Palmer (eds) *Race, Culture and Psychotherapy: Critical Perspectives in Multicultural Practice.* Sussex: Routledge.

Tew, J. (ed.) (2005) *Social Perspectives in Mental Health: Developing Social Models for Understanding and Working with Mental Distress.* London: Jessica Kingsley Publishers.

The 1990 Trust (2005) *London NHS Organisations Race Equality Schemes: Headline Reviews 2005.* London: The 1990 Trust.

Thoburn, J. (2005) 'Permanent Family Placement for Children of Dual Heritage: Issues Arising from a Longitudinal Study.' In T. Okitikpi (ed.) *Working with Children of Mixed Parentage.* Dorset: Russell House Publishing.

Thomas, L. (1992) 'Racism and Psychotherapy: Working with Race in the Consulting Room – An Analytical View.' In J. Kareem and R. Littlewood (eds) *Intercultural Therapy: Themes, Interpretations and Practice.* Oxford: Blackwell Science Limited.

Thomas, P. and Bracken, P. (2005) *Postpsychiatry: Mental Health in a Postmodern World: International Perspectives in Philosophy and Psychiatry.* Oxford: Oxford University Press.

Thorne, K. and Mackey, D. (2007) *Everything you Needed to Know About Training.* London: Kohan Page Ltd.

Tizard, B. and Phoenix, A. (1993) *Black, White or Mixed Race? Race and Racism in the Lives of Young People of Mixed Parentage.* London: Routledge.

TNS (2007) *Attitudes to Mental Illness 2007.* London: National Statistics Office.

Torrington, D., Taylor, S. and Hall, L. (2007) *Human Resources Management.* Essex: Financial Times/Prentice Hall.

Trevithick, P. (2005) *Social Work Skills: A Practice Handbook.* Maidenhead: Open University Press.

Tribe, R. (1999) 'Therapeutic work with refugees living in exile: Observations on clinical practice.' *Counselling Psychology Quarterly 12*, 3, 233–243.

Trivedi, P. (2000) 'Racism, Social Exclusion and Mental Health: A Black Service User's Perspective.' In K. Bhui (ed.) *Racism and Mental Health: Prejudice and Suffering.* London: Jessica Kingsley Publishers.

Tuitt, P. (2004) *Race, Law, Resistance.* London: Routledge.

Veling, W., Selton, J., Susser, E., Laan, W., Mackenbach, J. and Hoek, H. (2007) 'Discrimination and the incidence of psychotic disorders among ethnic minorities in The Netherlands.' *International Journal of Epidemiology 34*, 4, 761–768.

Waal, A. de (2007) *Strategic Performance Management: A Managerial and Behavioural Approach.* Hampshire: Palgrave Macmillan.

Walshe, K. and Smith, J. (eds) (2006) *Healthcare Management.* Maidenhead: Open University Press.

Ward, G. (2006) *Unforgivable Blackness: The Rise and Fall of Jack Johnston.* London: Pimlico.

Whitacker, R. (2004) 'The case against anti-psychotic drugs: A 50 year evidence of doing more harm than good.' *Medical Hypothesis 62*, 59613.

Williams, P. (1997) *Seeing a Colour-Blind Future.* London: Virago Press.

Wilson, M. (1993) *Raised Voices: Mental Health and Britain's Black Communities.* London: King's Fund.

Wing, J.K., Beevor, A.S., Curtis, R.H., Park, S.B.G., Hadden, S. and Burns, A. (1998) 'Health of the Nation Outcome Scales (HONoS). Research and development.' *British Journal of Psychiatry 172, 1,* 11–18.

Wiseman, H., Metzl, E. and Barber, J. (2006) 'Anger, guilt and intergenerational communication of trauma in the interpersonal narratives of second generation holocaust survivors.' *American Journal of Orthopsychiatry 76,* 2, 176–182.

Wright, B. (2006) *The Psychopathic Racial Personality and Other Essays* (2nd ed.) Chicago, IL: Third World Press.

Zeitlin, H. (2002) 'Adoption of Children from Minority Groups.' In K. Dwivedi (ed.) *Meeting The Needs of Ethnic Minority Children* London: Jessica Kingsley Publishers.

SUBJECT INDEX

AUTHOR INDEX